More pre-publication
REVIEWS, COMMENTARIES, EVALUATIONS . . .

"This collection of STATE-OF-THE-ART papers will be of considerable value to tourism practitioners and students alike, particularly those interested in the technical aspects of tourism demand forecasting. . . . . "This collection of STATE-OF-THE-ART papers will be of considerable value to tourism practitioners and students alike, particularly those interested in the technical aspects of tourism demand forecasting. . . . Brings together eight new papers that tackle the problems of tourism modeling and forecasting from a variety of perspectives. The methodological approaches include cointegration, seasonal autoregressive integrated moving average (SARIMA) models, cyber filters, structural integrated time series econometric analysis (SITEA), principal components and ridge regression, logistic learning curve models, and cohort analysis."

THHP

Dr. Peter Romilly
Senior Lecturer in Economics
University of Abertay Dundee
United Kingdom

Kevir
Haiy
Editors

130359

Tourism Forecasting and Marketing

— FOOD, TOURISM & CREATIVE STUDIES

Tourism Forecasting and Marketing has been co-published simultaneously as *Journal of Travel & Tourism Marketing*, Volume 13, Numbers 1/2 2002.

Pre-publication REVIEWS, COMMENTARIES, EVALUATIONS . . .

" **P**RESENTS NEW AND REFRESH-ING FINDINGS and syntheses from conceptual as well as empirically tested models that will be A VERY USEFUL SOURCE for students of tourism and practitioners as well as development and investment decision-makers in the private and public sectors."

Muzaffer Uysal, PhD
Professor of Tourism Research
Virginia Polytechnic Institute
and State University

More pre-publication
REVIEWS, COMMENTARIES, EVALUATIONS . . .

"A VALUABLE RESOURCE for policymakers in both the private and public sectors. . . . Makes a significant contribution to the field of tourism forecasting by bringing together many different research methodologies with data on tourism flows from around the world."

Pauline J. Sheldon, PhD
Interim Dean and Professor
School of Travel Industry Management
University of Hawaii at Manoa

"A PIONEERING AND INVALUABLE REFERENCE TOOL for academics and graduate students undertaking research in tourism demand modeling and forecasting. . . . ESSENTIAL READING for decision makers in both the public and private sectors. . . . A most useful and scholarly collection of empirical research of substantial quality . . . HIGHLY RECOMMENDED."

Dr. Christine Lim
Senior Lecturer
School of Tourism and Hotel Management
Griffith University, Australia

"HIGHLY COMMENDABLE. . . . A collection by internationally renowned experts in the areas of tourism forecasting and marketing. . . . Covers a wide range of forecasting methodologies, from timer series analyses to advanced econometric techniques . . . . Of considerable interest to practitioners and researchers."

Dr. Xiaming Liu
Senior Lecturer
in International Business
Aston Business School
Aston University
Birmingham, United Kingdom

"PROVIDES AN ILLUMINATING PERSPECTIVE on current tourism demand forecasting from the vantages of U.S., European, Australian, and Asian markets. . . . Details current approaches and furnishes valuable findings on the relative importance of various factors affecting international and domestic tourism demand. . . . Will aid marketers, planners, and researchers in accurately evaluating the future of tourism demand and implementing policies to expand their visitor markets."

Douglas C. Frechtling, PhD
Professor of Tourism Studies and Chair
Department of Tourism
and Hospitality Management
The George Washington University

Tourism Forecasting and Marketing

Tourism Forecasting and Marketing has been co-published simultaneously as *Journal of Travel & Tourism Marketing,* Volume 13, Numbers 1/2 2002.

The *Journal of Travel & Tourism Marketing*™ Monographic "Separates"

Executive Editor: K. S. (Kaye) Chon

Below is a list of "separates," which in serials librarianship means a special issue simultaneously published as a special journal issue or double-issue *and* as a "separate" hardbound monograph. (This is a format which we also call a "DocuSerial.")

"Separates" are published because specialized libraries or professionals may wish to purchase a specific thematic issue by itself in a format which can be separately cataloged and shelved, as opposed to purchasing the journal on an on-going basis. Faculty members may also more easily consider a "separate" for classroom adoption.

"Separates" are carefully classified separately with the major book jobbers so that the journal tie-in can be noted on new book order slips to avoid duplicate purchasing.

You may wish to visit Haworth's website at . . .

http://www.HaworthPress.com

. . . to search our online catalog for complete tables of contents of these separates and related publications.

You may also call 1-800-HAWORTH (outside US/Canada: 607-722-5857), or Fax 1-800-895-0582 (outside US/Canada: 607-771-0012), or e-mail at:

getinfo@haworthpressinc.com

Tourism Forecasting and Marketing, edited by Kevin K. F. Wong, PhD, and Haiyan Song, PhD, (Vol. 13, No. 1/2, 2002). *"A VALUABLE RESOURCE for policymakers in both the private and public sectors . . . Makes a significant contribution to the field of tourism forecasting by bringing together many different research methodologies with data on tourism flows from around the world." (Pauline J. Sheldon, PhD, Interim Dean and Professor, School of Travel Industry Management, University of Hawaii at Manoa)*

Japanese Tourists: Socio-Economic, Marketing and Psychological Analysis, edited by K. S. (Kaye) Chon, Tustomo Inagaki, and Taji Ohashi (Vol. 9, No. 1/2, 2000). *Presents recent studies on the socioeconomic, marketing, and psychological analysis of Japanese tourists.*

Geography and Tourism Marketing, edited by Martin Oppermann, PhD (Vol. 6, No. 3/4, 1997). *"Casts much light on how insights from geography can be applied to, and gained from, tourism promotion. . . . Well-written, informative, and interesting, and the issues are important." (David Harrison, PhD, Co-ordinator of Tourism Studies, School of Social and Economic Development, University of the South Pacific, Suva, Fiji)*

Marketing Issues in Pacific Area Tourism, edited by John C. Crotts, PhD, and Chris A. Ryan, PhD (Vol. 6, No. 1, 1997). *"A significant volume on the marketing issues that face the region. Nicely complements existing texts and will carve its own distinctive niche as a reference work. . . . Valuable to students of tourism marketing both inside and outside of the Pacific region." (C. Michael Hall, PhD, Professor and Chairperson, Tourism and Services Management, Victoria University of Wellington, New Zealand)*

Recent Advances in Tourism Marketing Research, edited by Daniel R. Fesenmaier, PhD, Joseph T. O'Leary, PhD, and Muzaffer Uysal, PhD (Vol. 5, No. 2/3, 1996). *"This book clearly marks the current advancement in tourism marketing research. . . . Tourism marketing researchers and academics can gain useful insights by reading this text." (Journal of the Academy of Marketing Science)*

Economic Psychology of Travel and Tourism, edited by John C. Crotts. PhD. and W. Fred van Raaij, PhD (Vol. 3, No. 3, 1995). *"A fresh and innovative volume that expands our understanding of consumers in the tourism market. . . . Will be a useful reference for scholars and graduate students working in tourism psychology and marketing." (Dr. Stephen L. J. Smith. Professor, Department of Recreation and Leisure Studies, University of Waterloo, Ontario, Canada)*

Communication and Channel Systems in Tourism Marketing, edited by Muzaffer Uysal. PhD. and Daniel R. Fesenmaier, PhD (Vol. 2, No. 2/3, 1994). *"Loaded with information on a variety of topics that provides readers with a solid background of the topic as well as introduces them to new ideas. . . . A valuable resource." (Robert M. O'Halloran. PhD. Associate Professor, School of Hotel, Restaurant & Tourism, University of Denver)*

Published by

The Haworth Hospitality Press®, 10 Alice Street, Binghamton, NY 13904-1580 USA

The Haworth Hospitality Press® is an imprint of The Haworth Press, Inc., 10 Alice Street, Binghamton, NY 13904-1580 USA.

Tourism Forecasting and Marketing has been co-published simultaneously as *Journal of Travel & Tourism Marketing,* Volume 13, Numbers 1/2 2002.

Cover design by Brooke R. Stiles

Library of Congress Cataloging-in-Publication Data

Tourism forecasting and marketing / Kevin K. F. Wong, Haiyan Song, editors.
     p. cm.
"Co-published simultaneously as 'Journal of travel & tourism marketing', vol. 13, nos. 1/2 2002." Includes bibliographical references and index.
     ISBN 0-7890-2086-6 (hard : alk. paper)-ISBN 0-7890-2087-4 (pbk : alk. paper)
1. Tourism-Econometric models. 2. Tourism-Forecasting. 3. Tourism-Marketing. I. Wong, Kevin Kai Fai, 1969- II. Song, Haiyan. III. Journal of travel & tourism marketing.
G155.A1 T59185 2003
338.4'791'0015195-dc21

                              2002153969

Tourism Forecasting and Marketing

Kevin K. F. Wong
Haiyan Song
Editors

Tourism Forecasting and Marketing has been co-published simultaneously as *Journal of Travel & Tourism Marketing*, Volume 13, Numbers 1/2 2002.

THHP

The Haworth Hospitality Press
An Imprint of
The Haworth Press, Inc.
New York • London • Oxford

Indexing, Abstracting & Website/Internet Coverage

This section provides you with a list of major indexing & abstracting services. That is to say, each service began covering this periodical during the year noted in the right column. Most Websites which are listed below have indicated that they will either post, disseminate, compile, archive, cite or alert their own Website users with research-based content from this work. (This list is as current as the copyright date of this publication.)

Abstracting, Website/Indexing Coverage . . . . Year When Coverage Began

- *Business Periodicals Index (BPI) <www.hwwilson.com>* **1999**

- *CIRET (Centre International de Recherches et d'Etudes Touristiques) <www.ciret-tourism.com>* **2000**

- *CNPIEC Reference Guide: Chinese National Directory of Foreign Periodicals* **1995**

- *Emerald Management Reviews (formerly known as Anbar Management Intelligence Abstracts) <www.emeraldinsight. com/reviews/index.htm>* **1998**

- *FINDEX <www.publist.com>* **1999**

- *Hospitality Research-At-a-Glance Index* **1998**

- *IBZ International Bibliography of Periodical Literature <www.saur.de>* **1995**

- *International Hospitality and Tourism Database, The* **1995**

- *Leisure, Recreation & Tourism Abstracts, c/o CAB International/CAB ACCESS <www.cabi.org>* **1993**

- *Lodging, Restaurant & Tourism Index* **1992**

- *Management & Marketing Abstracts* **1992**

(continued)

Special Bibliographic Notes related to special journal issues (separates) and indexing/abstracting:

- indexing/abstracting services in this list will also cover material in any "separate" that is co-published simultaneously with Haworth's special thematic journal issue or DocuSerial. Indexing/abstracting usually covers material at the article/chapter level.
- monographic co-editions are intended for either non-subscribers or libraries which intend to purchase a second copy for their circulating collections.
- monographic co-editions are reported to all jobbers/wholesalers/approval plans. The source journal is listed as the "series" to assist the prevention of duplicate purchasing in the same manner utilized for books-in-series.
- to facilitate user/access services all indexing/abstracting services are encouraged to utilize the co-indexing entry note indicated at the bottom of the first page of each article/chapter/contribution.
- this is intended to assist a library user of any reference tool (whether print, electronic, online, or CD-ROM) to locate the monographic version if the library has purchased this version but not a subscription to the source journal.
- individual articles/chapters in any Haworth publication are also available through the Haworth Document Delivery Service (HDDS).

Tourism Forecasting and Marketing

CONTENTS

ABOUT THE EDITORS

Kevin K. F. Wong, PhD, is Associate Professor of Tourism in the School of Hotel and Management, The Hong Kong Polytechnic Institute in Hong Kong, where he received the Outstanding Consultancy Award in 1998 for his contributions to the tourism industry. His scholarly publications include papers in the *Journal of Travel & Tourism Research* (Haworth), the *Journal of Travel Research, Tourism Management,* and the *Journal of Hospitality and Tourism Research.*

Haiyan Song, PhD, is Reader in Economics in the School of Management, University of Surrey in England. He is co-author of *Tourism Demand Modeling and Forecasting: Modern Econometric Approaches,* and his work has appeared in numerous academic journals, including the *Journal of Applied Econometrics,* the *International Journal of Forecasting,* the *Journal of Transportation Economics and Policy,* and the *Journal of Travel Research and Tourism Analysis.*

Introduction:
Tourism Forecasting:
State of the Art

Although much progress has been made in tourism demand modeling and forecasting over the last two decades, more research is still needed to address important issues relating to the concepts, model specification, data analysis and methodologies used in tourism forecasting. To fill this gap, this volume on Tourism Forecasting and Marketing is being published to bring together rigorous research in this area.

Research papers on specific topics focusing on tourism forecasting and marketing were invited from international researchers in the field. Particular attention was given to research using and comparing traditional versus modern forecasting techniques; evaluating current and past forecasting methods; modeling and forecasting destination choice; and evaluating the impacts of forecasting and marketing on tourism demand.

The eight papers included in this volume are authored by researchers from the United States, United Kingdom, Australia and Asia and all the papers have gone through a rigorous double blind reviewing process. They represent cutting edge research in their respective areas on tourism modeling and forecasting. The new and refreshing findings from the models and techniques used will have a notable impact on the existing and past literature and will be useful for guiding government and private sector tourism investment and development decisions and initiatives.

[Haworth co-indexing entry note]: "Introduction: Tourism Forecasting: State of the Art." Wong, Kevin K. F., and Haiyan Song. Co-published simultaneously in *Journal of Travel & Tourism Marketing* (The Haworth Hospitality Press, an imprint of The Haworth Press, Inc.) Vol. 13, No. 1/2, 2002, pp. 1-3; and: *Tourism Forecasting and Marketing* (ed: Kevin K. F. Wong and Haiyan Song) The Haworth Hospitality Press, an imprint of The Haworth Press, Inc., 2002, pp. 1-3. Single or multiple copies of this article are available for a fee from The Haworth Document Delivery Service [1-800-HAWORTH, 9:00 a.m. - 5:00 p.m. (EST). E-mail address: getinfo@haworthpressinc.com].

The first two papers deal with inbound tourism demand for China and Greece using time series models. To begin, Nada Kulendran and Jordan Shan examine the use of conventional seasonal ARIMA model with non-seasonal and seasonal differences to forecast overseas visitor arrivals to China and make the appropriate comparisons to other structural models to arrive at the best forecasting model. Following this, Panos Louvieris embarks upon a contingency approach and investigates the suitability of a multiplicative seasonal autoregressive integrated moving average (SARIMA) approach to forecast Greece's inbound tourism in the medium to long term horizon with an introduction to the use of a cyber filter as forecasting evaluation tool. Both studies took into consideration the impact of the 2004 and 2008 Olympics on tourism arrivals.

Major economic factors which singularly or jointly influence the flow patterns and changes in tourism demand to Asian destinations are investigated using econometric models by the next set of papers. The specifications of the models used in the study by Stephen Hiemstra and Kevin K. F. Wong are based on partial non-linear demand models which includes indicator or dummy variables to measure the effects of seasonality and known structural changes. Relative consumer price levels between Hong Kong and the countries of origin, either alone or adjusted by relative exchange rates are found to be important influences in explaining tourist flows among most of the countries studied, with Japan being an exception. In the same vein, Amy Y. F. Tan, Cynthia McCahon and Judy Miller found that the measure of the joint effect of the changes in exchange rates and relative prices also appeared to be a better indicator for the price variable for both destination countries, namely Indonesia and Malaysia. Tourist expenditure is another significant manifestation of tourist demand. Woo Gon Kim and Hailin Qu employ the principal component analysis and ridge regression to examine the factors that affect domestic Korean travel expenditure. The number of working hours per week and size of household are found to be significant factors influencing domestic travel spending among South Korean tourists and, notably, these variables are different from those in Western societies.

A novel and new integrative approach, which combines both time-series and econometric methodologies, termed structural integrated time series econometric analysis (SITEA) is used in the study by Stephen F. Witt and Lindsay W. Turner to forecast international tourist arrivals by source country market and destination region within China. As pointed out by the authors the success of this newly developed model will be judged in the future by its ability to generate accurate forecasts.

Another perspective is offered in the paper by Geoff L. Riddington, which poses the question as to whether time series or econometric methods forecast tourism demand accurately. Using data on British skiing in Europe, he develops a Mixed Model incorporating economic factors into a Logistic Learning Curve model to forecast the growth of the ski market from UK to Europe. His findings suggest that as the market matures over time, further economic information may assume dominance and should be accounted for in the modeling process.

Related to the issue pertaining to the effects brought about by the passing of time and the particular life experiences associated with different generations from different time periods, the final paper by Lori Pennington-Gray, Deborah L. Kerstetter and Rod Warnick demonstrates how the Palmore cohort analysis can be utilized for tourism forecasting. At present, there is very little research that documents the change in different generations' or cohorts' travel behavior over time. Using Palmore's triad method the authors are able to explain observable differences between and within cohorts of international travelers and make inferences as to what effects (age, cohort and period) best explained the differences.

It is anticipated that this volume will serve as a stimulus for further debates in this important area of tourism and marketing research. New modeling methodologies such as cointegration, error correction and the vector autoregressive (VAR) approaches and their applications to tourism demand forecasting deserve more attention in the future studies.

We would like to express our thanks to Professor Kaye Chon for inviting us to be his guest editors for this volume and for his continuous support and encouragement in the entire process of publishing it. In addition, we would like to thank all our academic colleagues worldwide for their contribution to the refereeing process.

Kevin K. F. Wong
Haiyan Song

Forecasting China's Monthly Inbound Travel Demand

Nada Kulendran

Jordan Shan

SUMMARY. China is currently expecting a growth in inbound travel demand as the result of China's "open door policy," participation in World Trade Organization (WTO), success in hosting the Olympics in Beijing in the year 2008 and political stability. This paper focused on two issues: (1) forecasting China's monthly inbound travel demand and (2) seasonality and seasonal ARIMA model selection for monthly tourism time-series. In this paper following seasonal ARIMA models were considered: the seasonal ARIMA model with first differences and 11 seasonal dummy variables, the conventional seasonal ARIMA model with first and the fourth differences. In order to select the best forecasting model, finally both seasonal ARIMA models were compared with the AR model with fourth differences, the basic structural model (BSM) and the naïve "No Change" model. In the one-step ahead forecasting com-

Nada Kulendran is Senior Lecturer, School of Applied Economics, Victoria University of Technology, Melbourne, Australia. Jordan Shan is Senior Lecturer, School of Applied Economics, Victoria University of Technology, Melbourne, Australia and Visiting Professor at Peking University, Beijing, China.

Address correspondence to: Nada Kulendran, School of Applied Economics Victoria University of Technology, Footscray Park Campus, PO Box 14428, MCMC Melbourne, 8001, Victoria, Australia (E-mail: Nada.Kulen@vu.edu.au).

The authors are indebted to Emily Sinclair who provided valuable research assistance to this paper. The helpful comments of Professor Ken Wilson are gratefully acknowledged, though the usual disclaimer applies.

[Haworth co-indexing entry note]: "Forecasting China's Monthly Inbound Travel Demand." Kulendran, Nada, and Jordan Shan. Co-published simultaneously in *Journal of Travel & Tourism Marketing* (The Haworth Hospitality Press, an imprint of The Haworth Press, Inc.) Vol. 13, No. 1/2, 2002, pp. 5-19; and: *Tourism Forecasting and Marketing* (ed: Kevin K. F. Wong and Haiyan Song) The Haworth Hospitality Press, an imprint of The Haworth Press, Inc., 2002, pp. 5-19. Single or multiple copies of this article are available for a fee from The Haworth Document Delivery Service [1-800-HAWORTH, 9:00 a.m. - 5:00 p.m. (EST). E-mail address: getinfo@haworthpressinc.com].

parison, the conventional seasonal ARIMA model with first and the fourth differences becomes the best forecasting model for both inbound foreign visitor demand and total visitor demand. This may be due to the nature of monthly seasonal variations in visitor arrivals, which is less marked. Our forecasts indicate that China foreign visitor arrivals and total visitor arrivals are expected to grow by 14% and 27% respectively from 2002 to 2005. *[Article copies available for a fee from The Haworth Document Delivery Service: 1-800-HAWORTH. E-mail address: <getinfo@ haworthpressinc.com> Website: <http://www.HaworthPress.com> © 2002 by The Haworth Press, Inc. All rights reserved.]*

KEYWORDS. Seasonal ARIMA modelling, BSM modelling, forecasting china tourism

INTRODUCTION

Tourism has become an important sector in many countries, and reliable tourism demand forecasts are important for government and business for planning and investment purposes. Now that Beijing has been awarded the 2008 Olympic Games there will be more interest in visiting China by foreign nations. For efficient planning, accurate short-term forecasts such as one-month or one-quarter forecasts are required by transport sectors such as airlines, shipping companies, railways, coach operators and hotel industries. For investment purposes, government and private sectors require annual forecasts. To forecast international tourism demand, time-series models, econometric models and "no- change" models are commonly used in tourism forecasting studies. In the past, to forecast annual tourism demand, Martin and Witt (1989) used exponential smoothing, trend curve analysis, gompertz, stepwise autoregression, econometric models and no-change models. To obtain short-term forecasts such as monthly or quarterly tourism forecasts, Kim (1999) and, Lim and McAleer (1999) used the seasonal Autoregressive Integrated Moving Average (ARIMA) model, Gonzalez and Moral (1996), and Kulendran and King (1997) and Kulendran and Witt (2001) used seasonal (ARIMA) models and basic structural time-series models (BSM), structural causal models, no change models, and error-correction models. In tourism demand forecasting comparisons (Martin and Witt (1989), Kulendran and King (1997), Kulendran and Witt (2001)) found that time-series models and the "no change" model generated more accurate tourism forecasts than econometric models.

During the past decade or so, several econometric models have been developed and estimated in the tourism literature to identify the relationship between tourist arrivals in a particular country and the factors that influence the arrivals. In previous studies, factors such as income, price, price of substitutes, real and nominal exchange rates, airfares, marketing expenditure and special events are considered the most important determinants. The advantage of using an econometric model for tourism forecasting is, that it not only provides income elasticity, price elasticity, etc. for policy analysis but also provides conditional forecasts. However, this paper is limited to time-series models because in general, time series models provide better short-term forecasts and due to limited availability of data such as airfares, etc.

Our main interest in this paper is to identify the appropriate seasonal ARIMA model to forecast monthly total visitor arrivals (denoted by T-visits) and monthly foreign visitor arrivals (denoted by F-visits). China monthly foreign visitor demand time-series and China total visitor demand time-series exhibit trend and seasonality. However, monthly seasonality is less marked in the series (see Figure 1 and Figure 2). To model monthly seasonal variation, two models can be considered: (1) the seasonal ARIMA model with non-seasonal and seasonal differences and (2) the seasonal ARIMA model for the variable in its first differences, in which seasonality is modeled with a constant and 11 seasonal dummy variables. Our primary motive is to identify the appropriate seasonal ARIMA model for the monthly China visitor arrivals series, which has a less marked seasonal variation. Finally, forecasting accuracy of these models is compared with BSM.

In the past, Kim (1999) used the seasonal ARIMA model with non-seasonal and seasonal differences to forecast monthly Australian outbound tourism. Gonzalez and Moral (1996) used both BSM and seasonal ARIMA to forecast international tourism demand for Spain. In the Gonzalez and Moral (1996) study, BSM outperformed the seasonal ARIMA model. Seasonal ARIMA models are fitted to stationarity time-series, which means the series has a constant mean and constant finite variance and differencing is an important issue in seasonal ARIMA modelling. BSM models are not popular in tourism forecasting, however, the advantage of using BSM is that stationarity and differencing are less prominent. The BSM approach assumes that time-series components, namely trend and seasonality, are not fixed or deterministic and they may change over time. The stochastic trend and stochastic sea-

FIGURE 1. Foreign Visitor Demand

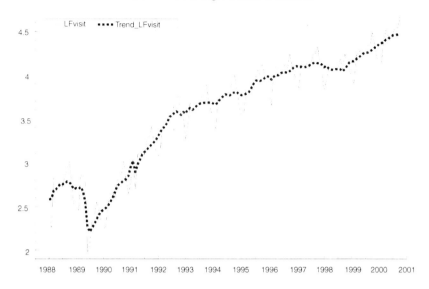

FIGURE 2. Total Visitor Demand

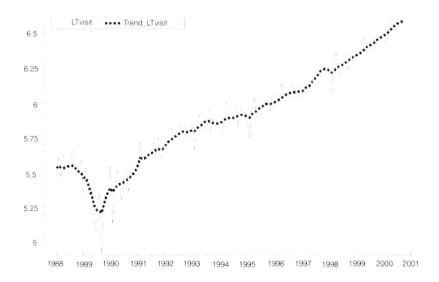

sonality included in the structural time-series model could capture the effects of all the socio-economic variables such as cultural differences, habits and tastes (popularity of the destination) that cannot be quantified. (Stamp 5.0, p. 53)

The plan of this paper is as follows: the second section discusses visitor arrivals to China and the growth; the third section discusses the seasonal ARIMA time-series models and the basic structural time-series model; the fourth section discusses the model estimation and forecasting; and some concluding remarks are made in the final section.

INTRODUCTION TO CHINA TOURISM

International tourism is important to developing countries as far as foreign exchange earnings and employment are concerned. International tourism is regarded as one important way of earning foreign currency. This notion has motivated several developing counties to adopt new measures such as investment in hotels, motels, transport and infrastructure, and marketing their tourism related goods and services overseas to further increase their overall international tourism market share.

In China, tourism is one of the most significant foreign exchange-earners (Wen and Tisdell, 1996 and Uysal et al. 1986). The number of visitor arrivals to China was insignificant until 1978 when China adopted the "open door policy." In 1978, the process of obtaining group tourist visa to China was eased and China International Travel Service (CITS) was allowed to market general tours through foreign operators, and work with them to design their own China programs (Bailey-EIU report, 1995). China's political stability and the economic reforms such as the support for market oriented activity, trade openness, special economic zones, the encouragement for foreign trade and investment and reforms in fiscal and monetary policies attracted more foreign investments into China. During 1981-1998, the annual growth rates of real GDP, external trade (both exports and imports) and tourist arrivals in China were 10 percent, 9 percent and 25 percent respectively. China's remarkable economic and trade growth over the last two decades has been accompanied by persistent inbound business travel to China. In 1998, business travel was some 55% of its total inbound foreign tourists to China. Business travel is very important as a catalyst to more general travel. Kulendran and Wilson (2000, p. 1002) stated "Increased business travelers may also lead subsequently to increased holiday and other travel when friends and relatives seeking adventure and recreation accompany business travelers. Moreover, the arrivals of products from other countries may lead to advertising and increased consumer interest in, and awareness of, both the product and the source country. This interest and awareness may lead to subsequent holiday travel flows in particular."

Since 1990, as a result of China's economic reforms and "open policy", China has become an important and fast growing tourist destination in the world. Table 1 provides some indication about China's rapid development in tourism.

According to the WTO, China was the 6th largest tourist destination in 1997 compared to the 18th in 1980. Its average growth rate during the 1980-97 periods was 12%, which is significantly higher than the world total (4.5%) and Asia's average rate (6.0%). At the same time, China was the top 8th tourist receipts earner in the world, compared to the 34th in 1980. Its average growth rate was 20% over the 1980-97 periods, which, again, is much higher than that of the world total (10%) and Asia (8.0%). China is the largest tourist destination and tourist receipts earner in Asia.

More foreign visitors visited China in the month of October due to the celebration of the founding of the Republic of China and good weather for touring. Seasonal variation in visitor arrivals can cause problems to the country such as low level of employment in the off-peak season and overcrowding and overuse of facilities during the

TABLE 1. Tourism in China: Some Indicators

	1980	1997
Tourist arrivals ('000):	3,500	23,770
% in world	1.22	3.9
% in Asia	11.2	27.1
Growth rate ('80-'97)	-	12%
Tourist receipts (US$ mil.):	617	12,074
% in world	0.59	2.77
% in Asia	5.4	15.7
Growth rate ('80-'97)	-	19.1%
World total:		
Tourist arrivals	285,997	610,763
Growth rate ('80-'97)	-	4.5%
Tourist receipts	105,320	435,981
Growth rate: ('80-'97)	-	8.7%

Source: World Tourism Organization, *Yearbook of Tourism Statistics,* 1999, pp. 13-14, p. 78 and p. 84

peak season. Total arrival pattern is peak in the month August, a traditional holiday month related to school holidays. A high growth in visitor arrivals to China increases the demand for tourism related goods and
services and in turn creates a demand for investment in hotels, motels,
transport and infrastructure. For planning and investment purposes, accurate forecasts of visitor flows to China are important. Now that
Beijing has been awarded the 2008 Olympic Games the need for more
accurate forecasts is even more imperative.

However, against this background, the tourism studies on China have
been limited, the noteworthy works are by Wen and Tisdell (1996),
Tisdell (1996), Shan and Wilson (2001) and Lew and Yu (1995). In the
past, few attempts have been made to forecast China inbound tourism
(see Turner and Witt, 2000). The forecasting methods used in this paper
will provide a new approach to tourism forecasting for China and it will
be an important contribution to the tourism forecasting literature.

SEASONAL TIME-SERIES FORECASTING MODELS

In this section seasonal ARIMA model and the basic structural model
are considered which are capable of modeling trend and seasonality.
The ARIMA model (Box and Jenkins (1976)) is a well-established
time-series model for short to medium term forecasting. The ARIMA
modeling approach expresses the current time-series value as a linear
function of past time-series values (AR), and current and lagged values
of a white noise process (MA). The seasonal ARIMA model, which can
be fitted to seasonal time-series (quarterly or monthly observations),
consists of seasonal and non-seasonal parts; the seasonal part of the
model has its own autoregressive and moving average parameters with
orders P and Q while the non-seasonal part has orders p and q. The number of seasonal differences used, D, and the number of non-seasonal differences, d, are to reduce the series to stationarity such that an ARMA
model can be fitted. In general, a seasonal ARIMA model is denoted by
ARIMA(p,d,q)(P,D,Q)^s.

In the seasonal ARIMA modelling, seasonal differences ($\nabla_{12} = (1 - B)^{12}$
where B is a backward shift operator) is used to remove seasonality (both
deterministic and stochastic). Non-seasonal differences ($\nabla_1 = (1 - B)$), is
used to remove trend (both deterministic and stochastic). The reason for
using the operator $\nabla_1 \nabla_{12}$ is that the sample autocorrelation of the series
transformed by the operator $\nabla_1 \nabla_{12}$ shows a much more interpretable
pattern and as such a parsimonious seasonal ARIMA model could be

fitted to monthly series. Most of the economic variables have non-stationary stochastic trend require the first differencing to remove the trend. Many time-series have deterministic seasonal patterns and do not require seasonal differencing if seasonal dummies can be incorporated into seasonal ARIMA models. If monthly seasonal variation is purely deterministic the traditional approach of seasonal differencing could over-difference the series. Unit root tests could be used to determine the seasonal differences (Franses (1991), Kim (1999)), however, the unit root test lacks power (Schwert (1989)). Previous studies (Kulendran and King (1997)) and Franses (1991, p. 207) indicated "correctly taking account of the type of seasonality and non-stationarity in monthly data can improve forecasting performance." Therefore, in this paper, to construct seasonal ARIMA models we considered a range of differencing: (a) First differencing (∇_1) with seasonal dummy variables (11 seasonal dummy variables), (b) Twelfth differencing (∇_{12}) and (c) First and Twelfth differencing ($\nabla_1\nabla_{12}$).

The BSM model introduced by Harvey and Todd (1983), assumes that a time-series possesses some structure, which is the sum of independent trend seasonal and irregular components. Let Y_t be the observed variable. The basic structural model has the form $Y_t = \mu_t + \gamma_t + a_t$, where μ_t, γ_t and a_t are trend, seasonal and irregular components respectively and a_t is assumed to be white noise. The deterministic trend component μ_t can be represented by $\mu_t = \alpha + \beta T$, where α and β denote the level and slope, respectively and T is the time trend (T = 1,2. . .N). The above model assumes that the time-series have a deterministic (global) trend and the slope (β) is fixed throughout time. Now we introduce the stochastic trend and stochastic seasonality as follows. The change in trend ($\mu_{t-1} - \mu_{t-1} = \beta$) from one period to another is the slope of the parameter β. If the stochastic terms (η_t and ξ_t) are introduced it is possible to replace the deterministic trend with a stochastic trend i.e. $\mu_t = \mu_{t-1} + \beta_{t-1} + \eta_t$ and $\beta_t = \beta_{t-1} + \xi_t$. where η_t and ξ_t are normally independent white noise process with zero mean and variances σ^2_η and σ^2_ξ. The effect of η_t is to allow the level of the trend to shift up and down while the ξ_t allows the slope to change. The larger value of variances σ^2_η and σ^2_ξ indicates greater stochastic movements and for deterministic trend the variance $\sigma^2_\eta = \sigma^2_\xi = 0$. If the seasonal effects are allowed to change over time, then the stochastic seasonal form is $\gamma_t = -\sum \gamma_{t-j} + w_t$, where w_t is a normally distributed independent white noise process with zero mean and the variance is σ^2_{wt}. If $\sigma^2_\eta = \sigma^2_\xi = \sigma^2_w = 0$, the structural model collapses to standard regression model with a linear deterministic time trend and constant seasonal patterns.

MODEL ESTIMATION AND FORECAST COMPARISON

Data for T-visits (in 10,000 persons) and F-visits (F) (in 1,000 persons) were obtained from *China Monthly Statistics*, published by China Statistics and Information Consultancy Service Center, State Bureau of Statistics, China. The data after 1999 was obtained from *The Latest Monthly Statistics*, published by the National Bureau of Statistics, China. The term F-visits means all those traveling on non-Chinese passports, except holders of Hong Kong, Macau and Republic of China (Taiwan) passports and travel documents. F-visits include ethnic Chinese who travel on passports other than those from Hong Kong, Macau and Taiwan.

Forecasting models identification, estimation and diagnostic testing were carried out over the period 1988(1) to 2000(10). The log transformation was considered to satisfy the assumption of constant error variance. First, the seasonal ARIMA models (denoted ARIMA1,12) considering first and seasonal differencing were fitted to T-visits and F-visits. The identified ARIMA^{1,12} models for F-visits and T-visits were ARIMA $(0,1,0)$ $(0,1,2)^{12}$ and ARIMA$(1,1,0)(0,1,2)^{12}$ respectively. An alternative approach in seasonal ARIMA modeling is to take the first differences and use eleven (11) seasonal dummy variables to model the seasonality and finally fit a seasonal ARMA model to the residual term that remains. For F-visits and T-visits, the identified ARIMA^{1} models were ARIMA$(0,1, 1)(0,0,0)^{12}$. In the ARIMA^{1,12} and ARIMA^{1} models, estimated coefficients are statistically significant (see the reported t values).

Estimated Seasonal ARIMA^{1,12} Model

F-Visit: $\nabla_1 \nabla_{12}$lnF-Visit = $-0.0036 + (1 - 0.451B^1)(1 - 0.505^{12})\varepsilon_t$
　　　　　　　　　　(t = -0.04)　　(t = -5.39)　　(t = -5.88)

T-Visit: $(1+ 0.290B^1)\nabla_1\nabla_{12}$ln T-Visit = $0.002 + (1 - 0.383B^1)(1 - 0.747B^{12})\varepsilon_t$
　　　　　　　　(t = 1.97)　　　　(t = 1.31)　(t = -11.5)　(t = -2.70)

Estimated Seasonal ARIMA^{1} Model with 11 Seasonal Dummy Variables

F-Visit: ∇_1lnF-Visit = $0.0118 + (1 - 0.402B^1)\varepsilon_t$ + seasonal dummy variables
　　　　　　　　(t = 2.01)　　　(t = -4.75)

T-Visit: ∇_1lnT-Visit = $0.006 + (1 - 0.558B^1)\varepsilon_t$ + seasonal dummy variables
　　　　　　　(t = 1.96)　(t = -7.28)

Another approach is to use seasonal differences by itself in seasonal ARIMA modeling. However, Harvey (1990) indicated that seasonal differences by itself in seasonal ARIMA modeling could lead to wide range of inappropriate ARMA models. The pure autoregressive (denoted AR^{12}) models were fitted to seasonal differences time-series to select the order (p) of pure AR process we used the Schwarz Bayesian Criterion (SBC) for each series from the range $p = 1...12$. For F-visits AR(1) and T-visit s AR(2) models were chosen by SBC. The estimated seasonal ARIMA models, AR(1) and AR(2) models error terms satisfy the assumption of independent error terms. The calculated p-value of the Chi-square test is greater than 0.05, therefore, we could not reject the null hypothesis that the error terms are independent.

The STAMP(5.0) (Koopman et al., 1995) program was used to estimate the BSM models and the result of the estimated variance of trend, slope and seasonality are given in the Table 2.

For both F-visits and T-visits the estimated value of $\sigma^2_\zeta = 0$ indicates the slope is constant and for T-visits $\sigma^2_w = 0$ indicates within sample stochastic seasonal variation is not significant or seasonal pattern maybe constant. The estimated BSM models error terms are independent. Reported serial correlation at the 1st and 9th lag is not different from zero and the Durbin-Watson statistics is closer to 2. In regression analysis, the measure of goodness of fit is represented by the coefficient of determination R^2, however it is not very useful for BSM model because time series exhibits strong upwards trends and seasonal cycle. Harvey (1990, p. 268) provided the appropriate goodness of fit criteria Rsy, for a series with trend and seasonal. For both models the estimated Rsy values are positive and models valid for forecasting.

The estimated BSM, AR^{12}, $ARIMA^{1,12}$, $ARIMA^1$ were used to generate one-step ahead forecasts for the post-sample period 2001(1) to 2001(12). One-step-ahead forecasts were calculated with re-estimation method and compared with the actual values of the series. In addition, the naïve "no-change model" ($F_t = Y_{t-12}$) forecasts were also calculated to compare with these statistical forecasting models. Forecasting accuracy was assessed using the mean absolute percent-

TABLE 2. Estimated Variance of Disturbances

	σ^2_η	σ^2_ζ	σ^2_w	Rsy
F-Visit	$0.45 * 10^2$	0	$0.38 * 10^5$	$0.26 * 10^1$
T-Visit	$0.12 * 10^2$	0	0	0.27

age error (MAPE) and root mean square percentage error (RMSPE). Each of these measures was used to rank the four forecasting models and the results for individual visits are presented in Appendix 1. In the one-month ahead forecast comparison, for both F-visits and T-visits, the ARIMA[1,12] model is the best forecasting model based on the measure of accuracy MAPE and RMSPE. Figures 1 and 2 have illustrated this. Forecasts from ARIMA[1,12] model are reported in Tables 3 and 4 and Figures 3 and 4.

CONCLUSION

This paper shows that the conventional seasonal ARIMA model with non-seasonal and seasonal differences is the best forecasting model to forecasts both China foreign visitor arrivals and total visitor arrivals. In the forecasting comparison, seasonal ARIMA model with first differences and 11 seasonal dummy variables did not perform well possibly because the seasonal effect is not that strong in the China visitor arrivals series. Seasonal variation in China monthly inbound total and foreign visitor demand explains only 44% of the total variation in monthly growth rate. The study by Osborn et al. (1999) indicates that only first

TABLE 3. Forecast from Seasonal ARIMA[1,12] Model and Forecasts of Annual Growth Rate

Year	Total Visits Forecast (0000's)	Foreign Visits Forecast (0000's)	Total Visits % Change	Foreign Visits % Change
2001	9,963	1,173	-	-
2002	12,169	1,341	22.14	14.35
2003	15,163	1,533	24.59	14.29
2004	19,270	1,752	27.09	14.24
2005	24,982	2,000	27.09	14.19

TABLE 4. Forecasts of Monthly Average Growth Rate

Visits	Jan	Feb	Mar	April	May	June	July	Aug	Sep	Oct	Nov	Dec
T-Visits	4.34	3.14	9.35	12.80	-8.93	-0.29	10.34	5.68	8.06	8.14	-0.78	5.35
F-Visits	8.29	-2.02	31.34	6.91	-2.26	-3.91	2.64	10.50	-2.28	14.22	-13.58	-11.87

Note: Total visitor arrivals monthly growth rate will be high in July and April and foreign visitor arrivals will be high in March and October.

FIGURE 3. Actual versus Forecast Total Visits

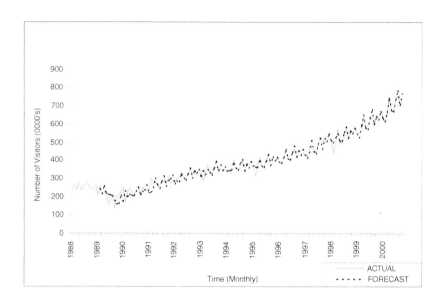

FIGURE 4. Actual versus Forecast Foreign Visits

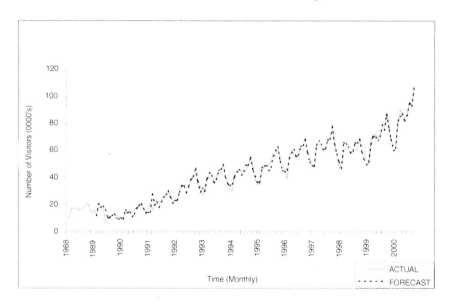

differences models appear to be most accurate at short horizons for series where seasonality is particularly marked. In the forecasting comparison "no change" model did perform worse than other models may be also due to the changing nature of seasonal variation in the post sample period.

The overall forecasts indicated that China foreign visitor arrivals will grow annually on average 14% and total visitor arrivals will grow annually on average 25% up to year 2005. However, Asia Pacific Tourism Forecasts 2000-2004 reported an annual foreign visit growth forecast value of 5.8% in 2004 (Turner and Witt, 2000). The expected high annual growth in China foreign visitor arrivals and total visitor arrivals may be seen as the results of China's increased openness to international tourism including tourism related to bilateral trade agreements between China and southeast Asian countries, USA and Australia and an increase in the awareness of China due to more openness to international trade. In the period prior to the Beijing Olympics in 2008, increasing accuracy in forecast ability will become vital if China is to reap the tourism opportunities associated with the Olympics. On the one hand China will not want to overestimate tourism interest since this will lead to wasted investment in infrastructure related to tourism. On the other hand China will not want to underestimate tourism flows to China because it will put undue pressure on existing infrastructure and tourism related prices and will inevitability impact upon consumers' perceptions of the tourism experience. Therefore, the ability to provide accurate forecasts of tourism flows will become increasingly important in the coming period. This paper has suggested that the conventional ARIMA model with non-seasonal and seasonal differences may prove efficacious as a forecasting tool.

REFERENCES

Bailey, M. (1995). China. *EIU International Tourism Reports*, 1: 19-37.

Box, G.E.P. & Jenkins, G.M.(1976). Time Series Analysis: Forecasting and Control. Revised Ed. Holden-Day, San Francisco.

China Statistical Yearbook & CD-Rom.China Monthly Statistics. (1999). China Statistics and Information Centre: Beijing.

Franses, P.H. (1991). Seasonality, Non-Stationarity and the Forecasting of Monthly Time Series. *International Journal of Forecasting*, 7: 199-208.

Gonzalez, P. & Moral, P. (1995). An Analysis of the International Tourism Demand in Spain. *International Journal of Forecasting*, 11: 233-251.

Gonzalez, P. & Moral, P. (1996). Analysis of Tourism Trends in Spain. *Annals of Tourism Research*, 23(4): 739-754.

Harvey, A.C. (1990). Forecasting, Structural Time Series Models and the Kalman Filter,Wiltshire: Cambridge University Press.

Harvey, A.C. & Todd, P.M.J. (1983). Forecasting Economic Time Series with Structural and Box-Jenkins Models: A Case Study. *Journal of Business and Economic Statistics*, 1: 299-314.

Kim, J.H. (1999). Forecasting Monthly Tourist Departures from Australia. *Tourism Economics*, 5(3): 277-291.

Koopman, S.J. Harvey, A.C., Doornik, J.A., & Shephard, N. (1995). Stamp 5.0-Structural Time Series Analyzer, Modeller and Predictor. London: Chapman & Hall.

Kulendran, N. (1996). Modelling Quarterly Tourist Flows to Australia Using Cointegration Analysis. *Tourism Economics*, 2(3): 203-222.

Kulendran, N. & King, M. (1997). Forecasting International Quarterly Tourist Flows using Error Correction and Time-Series Models. *International Journal of Forecasting*, 13: 319-327.

Kulendran, N. & Wilson, K. (2000). Is There a Relationship Between International Trade and International Travel? *Applied Economics*, 32: 1001-1009.

Kulendran, N. & Witt, S.F. (2001).Cointegration versus Least Square Regression. *Annals of Tourism Research*, 28(2): 291-311.

Lim, C. (1997). An Econometric Classification and Review of International Tourism Demand Models. *Tourism Economics*, 3(1): 69-81.

Lim, C. & McAleer, M. (1999). A Seasonal Analysis of Malaysian Tourist Arrivals to Australia. *Mathematics and Computers in Simulation*, 48: 573-583.

Lim, C. & McAleer, M. (2001). Monthly Seasonal Variations-Asian Tourism to Australia. *Annals of Tourism Research*, 28(1): 68-82.

Lew, A. A. & Yu, L. (1995). Tourism in China: Geographic, Political, and Economic Perspective. Oxford: Westview Press.

Martin, C.A. & Witt, S.F. (1989). Forecasting Tourism Demand: A Comparison of the Accuracy of Several Quantitative Methods. *International Journal of Forecasting*, 5: 7-19.

Osborn, D.R. Heravi, S., & Birchenhall, C.R. (1999).Seasonal Unit Roots and Forecasts of Two-Digit European Industrial Production. *International Journal of Forecasting*, 15: 27-47.

Schwert, G.W. (1989).Tests for Unit Roots: A Monte Carlo Investigation. *Journal of Business and Economic Statistics*, 7: 145-159.

Shan, Jordan Z. & Wilson, K. (2001). Causality between International Trade and Tourism: the empirical evidence from China. *Applied Economics Letters*, 5: 234-238.

Tisdell, C. A. (1996).Tourism Development in China: its Nature, the Changing Market and Business Opportunities. *Journal of Vacation Marketing*, 2(2): 123-136.

Turner, L.W. & Witt, S.F (2000). Asia Pacific Tourism Forecasts 2000-2004. *Travel and Tourism Intelligence*: 90-93.

Uysal, M., Wei, L. & Reid, L. M (1986).Development of International Tourism in PR China. *Tourism Management*, 7: 113-119.

Wen, J., & Tisdell, C. (1996). Spatial Distribution of Tourism in China: Economic and Other Influences. *Tourism Economics*, 2(3): 235-250.

APPENDIX

Forecasting Accuracy of F-Visits and T-Visits

Forecast Horizon	Forecasting Method	F-visit		T-Visit	
		MAPE	RMSPE	MAPE	RMSPE
1-Step	ARIMA[1]	3.25(3)	0.38(3)	3.19(2)	0.34(1)
	ARIMA[1,12]	2.86(1)	0.36(1)	2.27(1)	0.34(1)
	AR[4]	5.20(4)	0.83(4)	4.34(4)	0.59(4)
	BSM	3.02(2)	0.37(2)	3.20(3)	0.34(1)
	No-Change	8.17(5)	1.19(5)	5.49(5)	0.67(5)

Note: The figures in parentheses denote rankings.

Forecasting International Tourism Demand for Greece: A Contingency Approach

Panos Louvieris

SUMMARY. Accurate tourism demand forecasting has an important role to play in underpinning government investment decisions concerning the development of national tourism infrastructure for future economic benefit. In this paper a contingency approach to tourism forecasting model selection is taken and the appropriateness of a multiplicative seasonal autoregressive integrated moving average (SARIMA) to modelling Greece's inbound tourism in the medium/long-term to the year 2005 is investigated. Furthermore, the findings of this paper indicate that there are circumstances where the conventional restriction and use of ARIMA for short-term forecasting only can be relaxed. Predicated upon the impact of previous Olympic Games on host nations' tourism demand, baseline shift estimates were incorporated to the SARIMA baseline time series model using simple superposition. Predicting the most likely level of inbound tourism demand in Greece, as a consequence of the forthcoming 2004 Olympic Games, inevitably has major

Panos Louvieris is Director of the Centre for eLearning Research in Management, Deputy Director of the Centre of eTourism Research and Lecturer in the School of Management Studies for the Service Sector, University of Surrey, UK.

Address correspondence to: Panos Louvieris, Centre for eLearning Research in Management, School of Management Studies for the Service Sector, University of Surrey, UK (E-mail: mss1pl@surrey.ac.uk).

[Haworth co-indexing entry note]: "Forecasting International Tourism Demand for Greece: A Contingency Approach." Louvieris, Panos. Co-published simultaneously in *Journal of Travel & Tourism Marketing* (The Haworth Hospitality Press, an imprint of The Haworth Press, Inc.) Vol. 13, No. 1/2, 2002, pp. 21-41; and: *Tourism Forecasting and Marketing* (ed: Kevin K. F. Wong and Haiyan Song) The Haworth Hospitality Press, an imprint of The Haworth Press, Inc., 2002, pp. 21-41. Single or multiple copies of this article are available for a fee from The Haworth Document Delivery Service [1-800-HAWORTH, 9:00 a.m. - 5:00 p.m. (EST). E-mail address: getinfo@haworthpressinc.com].

implications for government policy, tourism infrastructure investment and marketing decisions at various levels of aggregation. Within this context, two candidate SARIMA models are evaluated for their forecasting ability using conventional diagnostic statistics for goodness of fit together with comparisons made with alternative establishment forecasts. Whilst the limitations of univariate time series and SARIMA non casual models are acknowledged, within a contingency approach, the strategic implications of SARIMA to tourism forecasting and tourism marketing in data poor modelling contexts are nevertheless beneficial and insightful in the absence of more rigorous alternatives. Moreover, a systemic perspective is proposed where tourism forecasting and tourism marketing are considered to be integral components of a second order, homoscedastic, feedforward cybernetic model, i.e., a recursive cyberfilter approach (RCA). *[Article copies available for a fee from The Haworth Document Delivery Service: 1-800-HAWORTH. E-mail address: <getinfo@ haworthpressinc.com> Website: <http://www.HaworthPress.com> © 2002 by The Haworth Press, Inc. All rights reserved.]*

KEYWORDS. Tourism forecasting, ARIMA modelling, cyberfilter

INTRODUCTION

International tourism is a major contributor to Greece's national economy representing 30% of total demand. In 1992, short-term international tourist arrivals claimed 10% of total GDP compared with 8.5% for Spain and 8% for Portugal making Greece the highest ranking tourism country in the Mediterranean (EC Eurostat, 1995). In 2001, Greece still maintains this rank and is 15th place in the world classification of tourism. Tourism contribution to GDP in 2000 is estimated to be up to 7% (GNTO, 2001). The estimated number of tourist arrivals in 2000 is 12.5 million. A major catalyst in driving the enormous growth in international tourism demand for Greece over the past 30 years has been the promotion of affordable package holidays, where demand exceeded the country's population in 1994 registering 11 million tourists (Anastasiou, 1998). The overall average annual growth rate in the number of foreign tourists between 1980 and 1993 was 8% (Sakelariou, 1998). While this upward trend has been undeniably strong, it is nonetheless chequered with political and economic shocks that have acted as detractors on the growth of tourism demand;

such as, the two oil price shocks in 1974 and 1979, the Gulf War in 1991 (EC Eurostat, 1995), etc. Further testament to the fickleness of the tourism demand for Greece is illustrated by the sharp 19% downturn experienced during 1995 and 1996 in its EC primary market with a concomitant financial loss estimated at US$ 3.7 billion. On the other side of the coin, the emergence of the new eastern european market in recent years has been one factor that has attributed to smoothing out some of these negative impacts (Georgas, 1997). Another major compensatory factor underpinning growth in demand has been the low prices of the Greek tourism product. Furthermore, the relatively low per capita tourist spend is generally acknowledged to be due to the dominance of package tours holiday-makers, the lack of four and five star accommodation, and the largely passive and delayed marketing efforts of the Greek National Tourism Organization (GNTO). Clearly, government planning and policy concerning tourism infrastructure development and its ongoing management for controlled sustainable growth in tourism demand needs to be sensitive to influences of the above mentioned type; especially, when forecasting tourism demand to aid decision making. The arguments for justifying the need for the modelling of tourism demand are well rehearsed in the literature (Song & Witt, 2000; Witt & Witt, 1995; Athiyaman & Robertson, 1992; Morley, 1991; Archer, 1987; Uysal & Crompton, 1985).

This paper is primarily concerned with modelling and forecasting Greece's international tourism demand in the medium/long-term to the year 2005 that takes into account the impact of the 2004 Olympic Games. Within a contingency approach, multiplicative seasonal autoregressive integrated moving average (SARIMA) *time series* modelling is used.

The use of ARIMA modelling is normally recommended for short term forecasting, e.g., 18 months (Frechtling, 1996; Kulendran & King, 1997; Harvey, 1993). Another purpose of this paper is to demonstrate that ARIMA can also be used in both the medium and long-term for tourism demand forecasting and that imposing short-term artificial boundaries on forecasting horizon is arbitrary.

Moreover, as we move inexorably towards an eBusiness age which facilitates greater ease in the timely collection of current data, the use of SARIMA (or for that matter any other causal or non-causal model) as a recursive cyberfilter which links tourism planning and forecasting to operations is proposed.

SO, WHAT OF THE FUTURE?

Establishment forecasts from the Institute for Tourism Research and Predictions (ITRP) anticipates 14.1 million international tourist arrivals to Greece in 2004 and 14.5 million in 2005 with an average annual growth of 4% (Kouzelis, 1997). These forecasts are conditional upon the construction of 275,000 additional hotel bed-spaces and upgrading of existing tourism infrastructure, which are not necessarily guaranteed. Hence, it may just turn out to be wishful thinking or another academic paper exercise in practice. These forecasts (Table 1) were published before Athens was awarded the 2004 Olympic Games. This was a key scenario/impact which the ITRP forecasts did not take into consideration. The expectation that this event may have large and long lasting beneficial impacts on the pattern of international tourism demand will ultimately depend on the decisions made concerning the alignment of existing and future infrastructure investment with the marketing of this mega event.

Beyond any doubt, the 2004 Olympic Games can act as a magnet for thousands of foreign tourists. In fact, in the report of the Organizing Committee for the XXIX Olympiad it is stated that tourism is one of the first industries to benefit from hosting the 2004 Olympics. It has been estimated that in 2004 alone, revenues within the tourist sector will exceed US$ 140 million (Sakelariou, 1998). In terms of visitor numbers, the most optimistic projections involve half a million people visiting Athens during the period of the Games. Planners and organiz-

TABLE 1. Forecasts of International Tourist Arrivals to Greece to 2005

Year	International Tourist Arrivals (million)
1997	10.3
1998	10.9
1999	11.6
2000	12.6
2001	12.8
2002	13.3
2003	13.7
2004	14.1
2005	14.5

Source: Kouzelis, 1997

ers, however, take a more conservative stand and preparations are being made for 200,000 international visitors. In addition, the expectation is there for considerably more tourists throughout the 2004 Olympic year (Sakelariou, 1998).

A recent study of the 1996 Summer Olympic Games found the following: (i) the vast majority of spectators (92.5%) had not attended any other Games before; (ii) the most important factor that influenced the decision to attend was a "once-in-a-lifetime opportunity" (30%); (iii) expense was a minor concern (5%); (iv) the average participants age was 40; (v) the economic status of those likely to attend was skewed towards households with high incomes ($100,000+); and (vi) 22.5% of the respondents took side trips suggesting that regional tourism marketing should be part and parcel of an Olympic spectator marketing plan (Neirotti et al. 2001). From a marketing perspective, the 2004 Olympic mega event should be seen as part of an acquisition and retention strategy which provides the opportunity to cross-sell and up-sell other Greek tourism products. Olympic spectators are a much more affluent market segment than the traditional package holiday tourist which must surely have implications for decisions concerning Greek tourism infrastructure planning and investment.

Forecasting the impact of mega events on tourism demand are often erroneous and problematic (Hall & Selwood, 1989). For example, forecasts on visitor numbers to the Olympic Games of Tokyo and Los Angeles overestimated demand by 86% and 36% respectively (Pyo et al., 1988). Spain saw a whole percentage point reduction in tourism demand during the year of the Olympics (WTO, 1992). Similarly, forecasts for the 1987 America's Cup Defence in Fremantle were 22 per cent less than the 1.2 million predicted (Hall, 1992). At the time of writing this paper attendance figures for the Olympiad in Sydney were not available until the Organizing Committee publishes its final report in the latter half of 2001 (OCOG, August 2001).

Fortunately, the Olympic Games are not a "one-off" mega event and do exhibit some regular patterns to support a simple superposition to the 2004 baseline forecast for Greek tourism demand. This assumption is based on (i) *no-change*, at least for the next step, i.e., a four-year interval in the case of the Olympics, where there is strong evidence to support that the *no-change* model generates more accurate short-term forecasts than simple univariate time series and traditional econometric models (ECMs) (Witt & Martin, 1989; Sheldon, 1993; Song et al., 1999; Kulendran & Witt, 2001). In addition, the *no-change* model serves as a useful benchmark and best estimate in an area where there is a dearth of empirical evidence; and (ii) *once-in-a-lifetime opportunity*, as identified above from the Neirotti et al. (2001) survey, where 92.5% of the visitors were first-time attenders to the Olympic Games reinforcing the notion of a short, sharp impact on tourism growth (Sparrow, 1989).

With reference to Table 2, an estimate for the future impact of the 2004 Athens Olympiad on tourism demand is made. The most straightforward method of estimating the impact of the 2004 Olympics is to calculate the mean of the absolute number of international visitors to past Olympiads. In this case the mean was found to be 235,900 international tourists. Alternatively, an average of the percentages in Table 2 may be employed but as we shall see later breaks the no-change criterion on which the baseline shift assumption is founded. From a qualitative perspective, the similarities between Barcelona and Athens are strong in terms of climate, accessibility, both are major european tourism destinations, etc. Inspection of the International Visitors figures in Table 2 will confirm the *no change* criterion, a *naive forecasting* method (Witt et al., 1994), holds fairly well across the top three Olympic venues for which finalized figures were available. Furthermore, the fact that visitors to the Olympic Games consider it to be a once-in-a-lifetime mega event reinforces the argument for the absolute mean, not the percentage mean, to be used as the best estimate for the 2004 baseline shift on international tourism demand.

In taking a contingency approach to forecasting and model selection, careful consideration was given to the known circumstances, quality and availability of data as part of the due diligence for this research. The

TABLE 2. International Tourism Demand for Past Olympic Games

Venue	International Visitors	International Tourism Demand	%
Atlanta, 1996	210,000	1,251,650	16.8
Barcelona, 1992	235,400	39,638,462	0.6
Seoul, 1988	240,000	2,340,462	10.3
Los Angeles. 1984	400,000	1,552,671	25.7
Moscow, 1980	30,000	5,590,000	0.5
Montreal, 1976	300,000	13,016,759	2.3

Sources: The Organizing Committee for the Games of the XXVI Olympiad, *The Official Report of the Centennial Olympic Games*, Atlanta, 1996, Vol. 1; Georgia State Board of Tourism; F. Brunet, *Economy of the 1992 Barcelona Olympic Games*, Centre of Olympic Studies, Lausane; WTO Compendium of Tourism Statistics. The Organizing Committee for the Games of the XXIV Olympiad, *The Official Report of the Games of the XXIV Olympiad*, Seoul, 1988, Vol. 1; Korea National Tourism Organisation; Pyo et al. (1988); California State Board of Tourism; UN Statistical Yearbook; OECD, National and International Tourism Statistics.

forecasting model was constructed by combining, through simple superposition, two non-causal modelling methods; namely, the above mentioned no-change model and a univariate ARIMA time series model which is considered in the next section of this paper. The effect of the S11 dent has not been included in this paper because it is deemed that the air travel demand curve has fully recovered (Chisholm, 2002; Bray, 2002).

UNIVARIATE ARIMA TIME SERIES MODELS

Univariate ARIMA time series models are increasingly being used for *ex-ante* tourism demand forecasting, particularly in circumstances where the availability of data is limited (Dharmaratne, 1995; Song & Witt, 2000). Although non-casual univariate ARIMA time series models have criticized for their ambiguity and inability to address the determinants of tourism demand necessary for policy assessment, researchers (Lim & McAleer, 2000; Kulendran and King, 1997; Kulendran, 1996; Gonzales & Moral, 1995; Morley, 1993; Witt & Witt, 1992, Makridakis & Hibon, 1979) have shown them nevertheless to be extremely strong rivals to their causal ECM counterparts.

The *ARIMA model building method* as developed by Box and Jenkins (1976), which is also known as the *Box-Jenkins method*, is ". . . an empirically driven methodology of systematically identifying, estimating, diagnosing, and forecasting time series" (DeLurgio, 1998). Only a summary of the method is presented below. A full account of the procedures used in the Box-Jenkins method may be found in Box, Jenkins and Reisner (1994) or Delurgio (1998).

The Box-Jenkins method is concerned with iteratively building a parsimonious model that accurately represents the past and future patterns of a univariate time series. The method combines autoregressive, moving average, differencing/integration procedures and finally tests the model for statistical validity. The Box-Jenkins approach is normally implemented in four steps as indicated below:

- *Model Identification.* Autocorrelation functions (ACFs), partial correlation functions (PACFs) and descriptive statistics (Q-statistic) are the tools used to identify a tentative ARIMA model. According to the PACFs we can identify the seasonal pattern and difference the series to achieve stationarity in standard practice of ARIMA modelling.

- *Parameter Estimation.* Initial and final estimates are computed, so that the equation for the tentative model can be specified. (A general form of the Box-Jenkins ARMA (p, q) model is given by Equation (1)).
- *Model Diagnostics.* This stage involves checking the model for adequacy and goodness of fit. Residual analysis, which tests whether the model has white noise residuals that satisfy homoscedasticity conditions is the most important diagnostic check. If the tests are not statistically valid then the model has to be re-specified.
- *Forecasting.* If the model is satisfactory then trend and seasonality are re-introduced into the model and forecasts can be made.

$$Z_t = \delta + \phi_1 Z_{t-1} + \phi_2 Z_{t-2} + ... + \phi_p Z_{t-p} + e_t - \Theta_1 \varepsilon_{t-1} - \Theta_2 \varepsilon_{t-2} - ... - \Theta_q \varepsilon_{t-q} \qquad (1)$$

where

Z_t = the present observation;

$Z_{t-1}, Z_{t-2}, ..., \varepsilon_{t-1}, \varepsilon_{t-2}, ...$ = the past observations and forecast errors;

ε_t = the present forecast error;

$\delta, \phi_1, \phi_2, ..., \Theta_1, \Theta_2, ...$ = the constant and the parameters of the model.

The Box-Jenkins model is more complex in function and form and has more stringent validity tests and data requirements than other non-causal techniques. Generally, a minimum of sixty observations are required to build a good model (Delurgio, 1998), and just like ECMs there is no automatic procedure for remodelling as new data points are obtained for the time series. In addition, ARIMA model building is a customized modelling approach that is contingent on the uniqueness of the forecasting problem situation as manifested by its time series. Therefore, customisation is necessary if the ARIMA model is to achieve *requisite variety* (Ashby, 1956) with the forecasting problem situation under consideration.

With reference to the baseline forecast, the most important limitation is that the ARIMA methodology is not recommended for long-term forecasts (Kulendran & King, 1997; Harvey, 1993; Frechtling, 1996). However, the construction of ex post forecasts, which was undertaken in addition to the standard diagnostic checks, allows for considerable confidence to be placed on the final forecasts, provided that no major changes shall occur in the underlying pattern of international tourism demand for Greece. This condition is a moot point because, as we shall see later in the paper, the ARIMA modelling process employed in a re-cursive cyberfilter is self-correcting. A recursive cyberfilter approach does not impose arbitrary time horizons. Instead, the durability/time specificity of an ARIMA model is entirely dependent on its performance based upon its forecasting accuracy. Time series "well- behavedness" and stability is usually a necessary assumption for accurate demand forecast us-ing ARIMA models. Generally, short-term international tourist arrivals of-ten display strong seasonal patterns (Lim & McAleer, 2000) and this is confirmed later by the closeness of the ex post forecast to the actual time series for tourism demand. With the exception of the 2004 Olympiad mega event sharp shock, it expected that the international tourism de-mand for Greece is likely to follow past trends.

Data availability and collection is a further constraint on the choice of model building method. International tourism demand to a destina-tion is mostly measured in terms of the number of tourist visits and to a lesser extent by tourist expenditure (Lim & McAleer, 2000). Greece is no exception. This research was limited to a data set of validated and confirmed monthly figures for tourism arrivals from January 1981 to December 1997 supplied by GNTO, i.e., 204 observations. Clearly in this case we are dealing with a data poor modelling environment where the data on tourism demand is limited. Under these circumstances autoregressive modelling is considered to be a useful alternative for tourism demand forecasting (Song & Witt, 2000) and provides a further justification for selecting the ARIMA model building method.

In the next section we apply the univariate ARIMA modelling method described above to forecasting international tourist arrivals to Greece.

FORECASTING INTERNATIONAL TOURIST ARRIVALS TO GREECE

Baseline forecasts for international tourist arrivals to Greece are gen-erated in accordance with the steps of Box-Jenkins approach previously outlined. Initially, a general class of ARIMA models is identified after removing seasonality and trend from the time series. Model parameters are estimated for several models and competing models are subjected to diagnostic checking. Ex post forecasting is employed to test the fore-casting accuracy of the selected model. Next, an ex ante forecast is made and compared to some other establishment projections of interna-tional tourist arrivals to Greece. Finally, the impact of tourists attending the Olympiad 2004 mega event is superimposed to complete the demand forecast.

Determining a Tentative ARIMA Model

In applying standard ARIMA modelling, several mixed seasonal ARIMA (SARIMA) models were identified; but, after the diagnostic checks only two candidate models were retained for further examination. These models were selected because they performed significantly better than the rest in the diagnostic tests specified earlier. Both of them are SARIMA models of orders (7,1,7) $(0,1,1)_{12}$ and $(2,1,2)(0,1,1)_{12}$ respectively. Equation (2) describes the general expanded structure of the models:

$$(1-\phi_1 B-\phi_2 B^2-...-\phi_p B^p)(1-B)(1-B^{12})\ln y_t = \delta + (1-\theta_1 B-\theta_2 B^2-...-\theta_q B^q)(1-\Theta_{12}B^{12})\varepsilon_t \quad (2)$$

$\phi_1, \phi_2, ..., \phi_p$	= estimated coefficients of autoregressive terms;
$\theta_1, \theta_2, ..., \theta_q$	= estimated coefficients of moving average terms;
Θ	= moving average term of the seasonal component;
B	= backward shift operator;
y_t	= forecast variable;
ε_t	= error in time t;

SARIMA Model Coefficient Estimates

Estimates for the constant and the coefficients for the two SARIMA model equations are calculated using the Eviews (QMS, 2000) maximum likelihood estimation function. Apart from the constant terms, C, which are dropped since they are not statistically significantly different from zero ($t_c < 1.96$), all the other SARIMA coefficients for both models in Table 3 are significant at the 5% level of significance ($\alpha = 0.05$).

Using the estimated coefficients in Table 3 and substituting Y_{t-k} for $\ln y_{t-k}$ for $k = 2$ and $k = 7$, equations (3) and (4) for the two candidate SARIMA models are stated as follows:

SARIMA (7,1,7) $(0,1,1)_{12}$

$$Y_t = -0.4507Y_{t-7} - 0.4997\varepsilon_{t-1} - 0.419\varepsilon_{t-2} + 0.3063\varepsilon_{t-7} - 0.8097\varepsilon_{t-12} \quad (3)$$
$$(-5.6576)\ (-8.3472)\qquad (-2.2440)\qquad (4.5408)\qquad\quad (-19.3852)$$

SARIMA (2,1,2) $(0,1,1)_{12}$

$$Y_t = 0.166Y_{t-2} - 0.5689\varepsilon_{t-1} - 0.271\varepsilon_{t-2} - 0.7253\varepsilon_{t-12} \quad (4)$$
$$(2.0436)\qquad (-8.5288)\qquad (-3.3529)\quad (-15.4296)$$

The original time series may be obtained by utilizing the transformation given in equation (5).

$$y_t = exp(Y_t) \tag{5}$$

Diagnostic Checking

Having estimated the parameters of the two SARIMA models, the validity of the models' goodness of fit is assessed using diagnostic tests. The first test involves analyzing the residuals. If the correct model is fitted to the data, the expected values of the residuals will be statistically equal to zero, according to the ACF and PACF. The Q-statistic (Ljung & Box, 1978) for diagnosing "white noise" confirmed that the residuals were not statistically significantly different than those of white noise at the 5% level of significance for both models; in addition, the correlograms (not presented here) show their respective autocorrelations to be within the 95% confidence limits, i.e., patternless provement.

The two other diagnostic tests employed are the Akaike Information Criterion (AIC) and the Schwarz Bayesian Information Criterion (BIC) for selecting between competing models. The decision rule is to choose the model that minimizes the magnitude of AIC and BIC for a series. Investigations have shown that the BIC is the best individual determinant for achieving the best out-of-sample forecasting model (Delurgio, 1998). Moreover, the Schwarz BIC penalizes model complexity in line with the principle of parsimony. The R^2 statistic has not been used because it does not provide best guidelines for time series that have a strong upward movement (as demonstrated by the time series employed herein). In addition, the AIC and BIC provide a better balance of model complexity and goodness of fit than either R^2 or RSE (residual standard error), especially in situations where models exhibit high p and q values such as the SARIMA $(7,1,7)(0,1,1)_{12}$ model. Therefore, using the AIC and BIC criteria together with employing the principle of parsimony was the basis of the model selection between the two competing SARIMA models. Inspecting Table 3 and applying the AIC and BIC choice criteria, the SARIMA $(2,1,2)(0,1,1)_{12}$ is selected because it has the smallest values for AIC and BIC, and is the less complex model (low p and q values).

TABLE 3. Estimated SARIMA Models

	Coefficient	t-Statistic	AIC	BIC
SARIMA (7,1,7) (0,1,1)$_{12}$				
AR(7)	0.4507	5.658		
MA(1)	0.4997	8.347		
MA(2)	0.1419	2.244		
MA(7)	0.3063	4.540		
SMA(12)	0.8097	19.385		
C	0.000167	0.160		
Diagnostic Statistics				
			4.225	4.12
SARIMA (2,1,2) (0,1,1)$_{12}$				
AR(2)	0.166	2.043		
MA(1)	0.5689	8.529		
MA(2)	0.271	3.353		
SMA(12)	0.7253	15.430		
C	0.0002	0.338		
Diagnostic Statistics				
			4.202	4.116

Ex Poste Forecasting: Assessing the Forecasting Accuracy of the SARIMA (2,1,2)(0,1,1)$_{12}$ Model

There are many error measures available for assessing the accuracy of forecasts. Mean absolute percentage error (MAPE) and root mean square percentage error (RMSPE), are the two most common ones. In this paper MAPE is employed in an ex poste forecasting context to test the predictive power of the selected SARIMA (2,1,2)(0,1,1)$_{12}$ model. In order to assess the forecasts on an objective basis the scale proposed by Dharmaratne (1995) is applied where a MAPE of less than 10% indicates a highly accurate forecast, 10-20% is good, 20-50% is reasonable, and a MAPE of more than 50% indicates an inaccurate forecast. The MAPE is defined by equation (6):

$$\text{MAPE} = \frac{1}{m} \sum_{t=1}^{m} \frac{|\varepsilon_t|}{Y_t} \tag{6}$$

where m is the length of the forecasting horizon, ε_t is the forecasting error and y_t is the actual value in the ex post forecasting time horizon. The model estimation period is 1981 to 1990 and *m* is 7 years, i.e., withholding 84 data points for the ex post forecast. Applying the SARIMA $(2,1,2)(0,1,1)_{12}$ model to the truncated series yields an MAPE of 17% indicating the model is capable of producing fairly accurate long-term results, assuming the patterns of the past continue. Table 4 and the ex poste forecast graph (Figure 1) show a "good" fit, reinforcing its MAPE

TABLE 4. Ex Post Forecasts from Estimation Period 1981-1990

Year	Actual	ARIMA $(2,1,2)$ $(0,1,1)_{12}$
1991	8,271,258	9,319,932
1992	9,756,012	9,783,521
1993	9,913,267	10,203,004
1994	11,301,722	105,76,417
1995	10,712,145	10,897,495
1996	9,782,061	11,160,725
1997	10,588,489	11,361,502

Note: The forecast generated from the model is monthly, since the actual data is in the form of monthly international tourist arrivals. Yearly figures are simply summed monthly observations.

FIGURE 1. Ex Poste Forecast

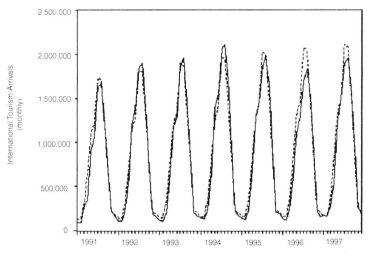

classification on the Dharmaratne Scale and provides further evidence to confirm the model's selection.

Ex Ante Forecasting

Having confirmed the validity of the SARIMA $(2,1,2)(0,1,1)_{12}$ model through the various diagnostic checks (AIC and BIC) and its acceptable ex post forecasting accuracy (MAPE), the model is now used to produce an ex ante forecast using all available time series observations. The ex ante forecasting horizon spans the period 1998 to 2005. In Table 5 the monthly forecasts are converted to annual figures by adding up monthly observations for each year; these are presented alongside the previously mentioned ITRP establishment forecast which assumes an unguaranteed expansion in the accommodation facilities in Greece.

In the case of the SARIMA $(2,1,2)(0,1,1)_{12}$ model, it is assumed that, first, there is no "out-of-character" infrastructure expansion/shock and, second, the model is defensible because the baseline ex ante forecast is grounded in its past behaviour/pattern. In order to overcome such discrepancies between alternative forecasts, a *Recursive Cyberfilter Approach* (RCA) which can capture emergent shocks is proposed in the next section.

In accordance with the previously developed arguments for including the 2004 Olympiad as a single year impulse on the out-of-sample ex ante forecast, the predicted international tourism demand for the Olympic year is 12,038,414 arrivals. This figure of just over 12 million com-

TABLE 5. Ex Ante SARIMA $(2,1,2)(0,1,1)_{12}$ and ITRP Forecast (in Millions)

Year	ITRP	Ex Ante SARIMA $(2,1,2)(0,1,1)_{12}$
1998	10.9	10.9
1999	11.6	11.2
2000	12.6	11.4
2001	12.8	11.5
2002	13.3	11.6
2003	13.7	11.7
2004	14.1	11.8
2005	14.5	11.8

prises of 11,802,514 arrivals predicted by the SARIMA $(2,1,2)(0,1,1)_{12}$ model plus the 235,900 baseline shift attributed to the Olympiad mega event.

A RECURSIVE CYBERFILTER APPROACH

It has long been acknowledged in previous studies conducted by the Centre of Planning for Economic Research in Greece that the need for regular, timely and accurate data from tourism essential services like hotels, car rentals, cruise shipping agencies, etc is a fundamental imperative for effective tourism policy development and infrastructure planning (Singh, 1984), including its subsequent management. The same sentiments are still echoed today by the GNTO in their stated objectives and measures to support information technology networks that facilitate data collection and statistical analyses (GNTO, 2001). IT networks and applications that are Internet-based provide the necessary infrastructure for the centralized data collection from Greece's geographically distributed tourism services. Furthermore the emergence of new eBusiness services from *application service providers* (ASPs), like Pegasus Solutions and Hoteltools.com, who offer affordable remote property management system services across the Internet to small and medium tourist enterprises (Pegasus, 2001; Hoteltools, 2001) will be a key enabler of public-private data sharing partnerships. The Internet and its associated digital technologies provide a common access IT platform which can enable national tourism organizations, such as the GNTO, to monitor the performance of tourism infrastructure investments, assess and control the impact of government tourism policy in their key tourism markets, in tempo with the dynamics of tourism demand at the point of consumption. In essence, what has just been described is a government-to-business (G2B) eBusiness cyberfilter.

In line with GNTO's marketing objective to diversify its tourism services portfolio for Greece's economic benefit, it is critical that any cyberfilter approach must be able to take into account ongoing and planned changes in the tourism services infrastructure, e.g., tourism infrastructure investment for the 2004 Olympic Games, if it is to be useful for forecasting purposes. Furthermore, a SARIMA time series model, or any other model for that matter, employed in a cyberfilter is at most an approximation of complex tourist behaviour which is not necessarily homogeneous through time. In taking a contingency approach to forecasting international tourism demand, a second order recursive cyberfilter (Figure 2) is proposed that links tourism planning and forecasting to operations.

From a cybernetics perspective, the second order recursion is the *intempo* remodelling of the SARIMA time series model, when necessary, so that the SARIMA model maintains *requisite variety* with its operational environment. In other words, the *Recursive Cyberfilter Approach* (RCA) allows the SARIMA model to be revised in order to reflect the new/most recent shocks/impacts on tourism demand as close as possible to the point of future interest. The question is: When to remodel? The maintenance of a viable SARIMA model, which is employed as the *predictor* in the cyberfilter, is contingent upon its forecasting accuracy as calculated by MAPE and/or RMSPE. In this paper we have used

FIGURE 2. Recursive Cyberfilter

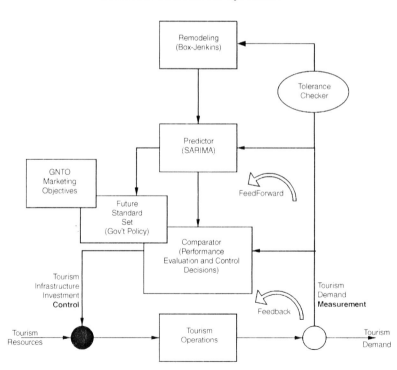

MAPE. The ability of a G2B eBusiness cyberfilter to synthesize data across *tourism operations* in-tempo with tourism demand means that as time progresses the number of observations available in the remodelling estimation period increases for an ex poste assessment of forecasting accuracy. The observations are gathered from *tourism operations* using the Internet enabled *sensor* (the white circle in Figure 2) in the cyberfilter to measure tourism demand. If the MAPE exceeds the specified acceptable forecasting error then the SARIMA model for future first order recursions is deemed to be unsatisfactory and therefore *out of tolerance*, at which point the second level recursion for *remodelling* kicks in. The MAPE is used in the *tolerance checker* of the cyberfilter. The *predictor* is part of the *feedforward* control in the cyberfilter and has two functions: first, it is used in this case to predict the future demand placed on tourism infrastructure/operations and set future objectives (the *future standard set*) on which to base government tourism policy; and second, it provides demand predictions for each of the tourism market segments to the *comparator* where deviation from the *future standard set* may result in corrective instructions for proactive action, concerning tourism infrastructure, to be taken via the *effector* (the black circle in Figure 2). Feedforward control in the cyberfilter is required to meet the GNTO's economic and strategic marketing objectives because it takes time to implement major infrastructure adjustments to tourism services, e.g., Olympic stadia, golf courses, marinas, large hotel complexes, etc. The final element, of the cyberfilter is a first order recursion concerned with the GNTO's short-term tactical marketing objectives/goals. This is the *feedback* control element in the cyberfilter. It is included for completeness in order to monitor and control short-term tactical influences, such as the impact of a pulsed advertising campaign, on tourism demand.

CONCLUSION

The use of the ARIMA model building method for short-term forecasting has been long acknowledged for its versatility and accuracy (Harvey, 1993; Frechtling, 1996; Delurgio, 1998). This paper sought to test the application and validity of the ARIMA method to the forecasting of Greek tourism demand in the medium/long-term. The findings of this research support the assertion that it is possible, at least within a tourism context, to build a parsimonious SARIMA $(2,1,2)(0,1,1)_{12}$ model with an acceptable MAPE (17%) for the medium/long-term forecasting of international tourism demand; this being contingent upon the continuation of the SARIMA $(2,1,2)$ $(0,1,1)_{12}$ model's patterns, exhibited during the ex poste forecast (Figure 1), into the future until 2005 i.e. throughout the ex ante forecast period. The SARIMA $(2,1,2)$ $(0,1,1)_{12}$ forecast is preferred to the ITRP establishment forecast because the ITRP is considered to be over optimistic given the GNTO's objective to increase the competitiveness of the Greek tourism product (GNTO, 2000) has not been achieved (Papathanasiou, 2001). Furthermore, key infrastructure investments to develop new alternative forms of tourism, such as marine and golf tourism, have yet to be implemented (GNTO, 2001; Kousounis, 2000). Therefore, the SARIMA $(2,1,2)$ $(0,1,1)_{12}$ has been employed in this paper as the baseline ex ante forecast for international tourism demand (Table 5). Indeed the findings herein have demonstrated that there are situations, sometimes, where the normally accepted restriction of imposing artificial short-term forecasting horizons on ARIMA modelling methods can be relaxed. Furthermore, the durability of a specific ARIMA model employed within the context of a cyberfilter is determined purely by error magnitude.

Using the principle of simple superposition, the impact of the 2004 Olympiad is treated as a single year impulse on the out-of-sample ex ante forecast and has been justified through evidence presented herein that supports the *no-change* model. In addition, the Olympiad is for most people a *once-in-a-lifetime* opportunity of who 92.5% are first-time attendees (Neirotti et al., 2001) reinforcing the simple baseline shift of 235,000 arrivals to tourism demand in the year of the Athens Olympiad, making a total of 12,038,414 tourism arrivals in 2004.

The challenge for the GNTO, which constitutes the Ministry of Development's ruling state agency for the tourism sector, is to manage a tourism infrastructure that is clearly in transition for Greece's economic and social benefit, and for the benefit of its tourists. In this paper a *Recursive Cyberfilter Approach* (RCA) has been proposed which leverages emerging digital technologies and the Internet, i.e., a G2B eBusiness cyberfilter, for the in-tempo management of tourism infrastructure investment planning and tourism operations. The main benefit and thesis of the RCA is its reflexive capacity to accommodate emergent shocks and to maintain a transitional tourism infrastructure in control as opposed to allowing it to drift.

REFERENCES

Anastasiou, B. (1998). Tourism: the Neglected Hope of the Greek Economy. *The Tourist Market*, March, pp 72-81. (In Greek).

Archer, B.H. (1987). Demand Forecasting and Estimation. In: Ritchie J.R.B. and Goeldner C.R. (eds.), *Travel, Tourism and Hospitality Research*. New York: John Wiley and Sons.

Ashby, W.R. (1956). *Introduction to Cybernetics*. New York: John Wiley.

Athiyaman, A. and Robertson, R.W. (1992). Time Series Forecasting Techniques: Short-term Planning in Tourism. *International Journal of Contemporary Hospitality Management*, 4(4), pp 8-11.

Box, G.E.P. and Jenkins, G.M. (1976). *Time Series Analysis: Forecasting and Control*. San Francisco: Holden-Day.

Box, G.E.P., Jenkins, G.M. and Reisnel, G.C. (1994). *Time Series Analysis, Forecasting and Control*. 3rd Edition, Englewood Cliffs, NJ: Prentice-Hall.

Bray, R. (2002). Inside Track Business Travel, *Financial Times*, Apr 16.

Chisolm, J. (2002). Companies & Finance UK: BAA. *Financial Times*, Apr 13.

DeLurgio, S.A. (1998). *Forecasting Principles and Applications*. Dubuque: McGraw-Hill.

Dharmaratne, G.S. (1995). Forecasting Tourist Arrivals in Barbados. *Annals of Tourism Research*, 22(4), pp804-818.

European Commission, Eurostat (1995). *Tourism In Europe*. Luxemburg: Statistical Office of the European Communities.

Frechtling, D.C. (1996). *Practical Tourism Forecasting*. Oxford: Butterworth-Heinemann.

Gonzales, P. and Moral, P. (1995). An analysis of international tourism demand in Spain. *International Journal of Forecasting*, 11, pp 233-251.

Georgas, V. (1997). The Bright Side of Tourism, *Capital*, July, pp. 40-44.

Greek National Tourism Organization (2000). *http://www.gnto.gr/3/04/0401/ec40101.html*. GNTO.

Greek National Tourism Organization (2001). *http://www.gnto.gr*. GNTO.

Hall, C.M. (1992). *Hallmark Tourist Events: Impacts, Management and Planning*. London: Behalven Press.

Hall, C.M. and Selwood, H.J. (1989). America's Cup Lost, Paradise Retained? In: Syme G.J., Shaw, B.J., Fenton, D.M. and Mueller, W.S. (eds.), *The Planning and Evaluation of Hallmark Events*. Avebury, Aldershot.

Harvey, A.C. (1993). *Time Series Models*. 2nd Edition. London: Harvester Wheatsheaf.

Hoteltools, (2001). *Hoteltools. http://www.hoteltools.com/company/about_ht.asp*.

Kousounis, S. (2000). Greek Tourism Loses Ground. *Kathemerini*, 21st December.

Kouzelis, A.K. (1997). *The Impact of Foreign Exchange Policy on Tourism Demand*. Athens: Institute for Tourism Research and Predictions.

Kulendran, N. (1996). Modelling Quarterly Tourism Flows to Australia Using Cointegration Analysis. *Tourism Economics*, 2, pp203-22.

Kulendran, N. and King, M.L. (1997). Forecasting international quarterly tourist flows using error correction and time series models. *International Journal of Forecasting*, 13, pp 319-327.

Kulendran, N. and Witt, S.F. (2001). Cointegration versus least squares regression. *Annals of Tourism Research*, 28.

Lim, C. and McAleer, M. (2000). A seasonal analysis of Asian tourism arrivals to Australia. *Applied Economics*, 22, pp 499-509.

Ljung, G.M. and Box, G.E.P. (1978). On a measure of lack of fit in time series models. *Biometrika*, 65, pp 297-303.

Makridakis, S. and Hibon, M. (1979). Accuracy of forecasting: An Empirical Investigation (with discussion). *Journal of the Royal Statistical Society*, A 142, pp 97-145.

Morley, C.L. (1991). Modelling Tourism Demand: Model Specification and Structure. *Journal of Travel Research*, 25(1), pp 40-44.

Morley, C.L. (1993). Forecasting Tourism Demand Using Extrapolative Time Series Methods. *The Journal of Tourism Studies*, 4(1), 19-25.

Neirotti, L.D., Bosetti, H.A. and Tend, K.C. (2001). Motivation to Attend the 1996 Summer Olympic Games. *Journal of Travel Research*, 39, pp 327-331.

Organizing Committee of the Olympic Games (2001). *Facts and figures on the 2000 Games of the Olympiad in Sydney*. OCOG.

Papathanasiou, J. (2001). The Ineffective Policy of the Government. *Anaptiksi*, Vol. 4, pp 38-41.

Pegasus Solutions (2001). *PegasusCentral: A Total Enterprise Solution*. http://www.pegs.com.

Pyo, S., Cook, R. and Howell, R. (1988). Summer Olympic Tourist Market-Learning from the Past. *Tourism Management*, 9(2), pp 137-144.

Quantitative Micro Software (2000). *Eviews 4.0: User's Guide*. Irvine, California: QMS.

Sakelariou, N. (1998). Athens 2004. *The Tourist Market*, November, pp 34-40. (In Greek).

Sheldon, P. J. (1993). Forecasting Tourism: Expenditure versus Arrivals. *Journal of Travel Research*, 32(1), pp 13-20.

Singh, B.P. (1984). *The Impact of Tourism on the Balance of Payments: A Case Study for Greece*. Athens: Centre of Planning and Economic Development.

Song, H. and Witt, S.F. (2000). *Tourism Demand Modelling and Forecasting: Modern Econometric Approaches*. Oxford: Elsevier.

Song, H., Witt, S.F. and Jensen, T. (1999). Forecasting performance of tourism demand models: the case of Denmark. Paper presented at the 19th International Symposium on Forecasting. Washington D.C.

Sparrow, M. (1989). A Tourism Planning Model for Hallmark Events. In: Syme G.J., Shaw, B.J., Fenton, D.M. and Mueller, W.S. (eds.), *The Planning and Evaluation of Hallmark Events*. Avebury, Aldershot.

Uysal, M. and Crompton, J.L. (1985). An Overview of Approaches Used to Forecast Tourism Demand. *Journal of Travel Research*, Spring, pp 7-15.

Witt, S.F. and Martin, C.A. (1989). Demand Forecasting in Tourism and Recreation. In: Cooper, C.P. (ed.), *Progress in Tourism, Recreation and Hospitality Management*, Vol. 1, London: Belhaven Press, pp 3-39.

Witt, S.F. and Witt, C.A. (1992). *Modelling and Forecasting Demand in Tourism*. Academic Press.

Witt, S.F. and Witt, C.A. (1995). Forecasting Tourism Demand: A review of Empirical Research. *International Journal of Forecasting*, 11, pp 447-475.

Witt, S.F., Witt, C.A. and Wilson, N. (1994). Forecasting International Tourist Flows. *Annals of Tourism Research*, 21(3), pp 612-628.

World Tourism Organization (1988). *Compendium of Tourism Statistics*. Madrid: WTO.

World Tourism Organization (1992). *Compendium of Tourism Statistics*. Madrid: WTO.

World Tourism Organization (2001). *Compendium of Tourism Statistics*. Madrid: WTO.

Factors Affecting Demand
for Tourism in Hong Kong

Stephen Hiemstra
Kevin K. F. Wong

SUMMARY. This study developed a set of seven demand models that identify the major factors associated with changes in tourism to Hong Kong. They included a model for each of the major countries that provide Hong Kong's incoming tourists. The significant parameters include those measures commonly used to assess the financial crisis that hit Asia in 1997-1998: gross domestic product, relative consumer prices, exchange rates, and interest rates. But, some other factors such as the change in Hong Kong sovereignty and seasonality were also found to be very significant. *[Article copies available for a fee from The Haworth Document Delivery Service: 1-800-HAWORTH. E-mail address: <getinfo@haworthpressinc.com> Website: <http://www.HaworthPress.com> © 2002 by The Haworth Press, Inc. All rights reserved.]*

Stephen Hiemstra is Professor Emeritus in the Hospitality and Tourism Management Department, Purdue University, West Lafayette, IN USA. Kevin K. F. Wong is Associate Professor in the School of Hotel and Tourism Management, The Hong Kong Polytechnic University, Hong Kong.

Address correspondence to: Stephen Hiemstra, Hospitality and Tourism Management Department, Purdue University, West Lafayette, IN 47906 (E-mail: shiemstras@ starpower.net).

This project was funded by a grant from the School of Hotel & Tourism Management, Hong Kong Polytechnic University, Kowloon, Hong Kong, for which the authors are very grateful.

[Haworth co-indexing entry note]: "Factors Affecting Demand for Tourism in Hong Kong." Hiemstra, Stephen, and Kevin K. F. Wong. Co-published simultaneously in *Journal of Travel & Tourism Marketing* (The Haworth Hospitality Press, an imprint of The Haworth Press, Inc.) Vol. 13, No. 1/2, 2002, pp. 43-62; and: *Tourism Forecasting and Marketing* (ed: Kevin K. F. Wong and Haiyan Song) The Haworth Hospitality Press, an imprint of The Haworth Press, Inc., 2002, pp. 43-62. Single or multiple copies of this article are available for a fee from The Haworth Document Delivery Service [1-800-HAWORTH, 9:00 a.m. - 5:00 p.m. (EST). E-mail address: getinfo@haworthpressinc.com].

KEYWORDS. Tourist arrivals, gross domestic product, consumer price index, exchange rates

OBJECTIVES

The overall objective of this paper was to identify the major contributing factors affecting the levels of tourism to Hong Kong during most of the decade of the 1990s. These impacts are measured in terms of changes in number of tourist arrivals from the major countries to Hong Kong. These factors are useful in understanding the nature and the size of the effects on tourism of the Asian financial crisis that began in late 1997 and carried through 1998. Relevant financial data are used as explanatory variables in a set of behavioural demand models. Non-economic factors included the change in sovereignty of Hong Kong that occurred in July 1997 and monthly seasonal factors. These models are expected to be useful for purposes of developing future projections, but that use is secondary to the objective of identifying the nature and size of the important behavioural characteristics affecting tourism.

BACKGROUND

Tourism is one of the most important businesses in Hong Kong, accounting for 6-8 percent of Gross Domestic Product for many years. In 1996, tourism became the second largest foreign exchange earner, generating HK$75 billion (approximately $7.75 per U.S. dollar) in revenue for the economy. It accounted for 7.9 percent of value added to Hong Kong's Gross Domestic Product, according to the Hong Kong Tourist Association (1996). However, the industry began suffering sharp declines in number of tourists in mid-1997, and there were important shifts in the origin of these visitors. Following growth of 5.2 percent during the first half year, tourist arrivals dropped 25.2 percent below year-earlier levels during the second half. Tourist arrivals dropped below year-earlier levels first in June of 1997 and for the entire year, averaged 11 percent lower. The decline was particularly noteworthy in view of the strong uptrends in tourism that had existed in recent years.

In 1998, the decline continued, and averaged 8 percent lower for the year. The decline was led by Japan, Korea, Thailand, Indonesia, and Philippines that each dropped by 30-50 percent from a year earlier in number of tourist arrivals. These declines were tempered by a 13-percent increase from Mainland China and a 2-percent gain from Taiwan. But, during the first quarter of 1999, the tide began to turn. Small increases were recorded in the overall number of tourism arrivals from most individual countries. The increase was led by a significant gain of 42 percent from Mainland China and 57 percent from depressed levels for South Korea during January-February.

The decline in number of tourists travelling to Hong Kong has been attributed importantly to the deteriorating economic situation in several of the countries from which Hong Kong draws its tourists. However, a survey by Plog Research Inc. suggested that Japanese tourists had become disenchanted with Hong Kong because of the high prices charged (1997). Taiwan tourists were said to be looking for new and different destinations. Some tourists indicated that other destinations simply had more current appeal.

The regional economic deterioration was expressed in currency depreciations that began in Thailand in fall 1997 and quickly spread to Malaysia, Korea, and Indonesia. The Thai government "floated" their currency, the baht, on July 4, 1997, by removing its previous "peg" (since 1986) to the U.S. dollar. It dropped precipitously in value thereafter triggered by Thailand's ballooning current account deficit and speculative sales. As early as August, the International Monetary Fund (IMF) had provided standby loans to bolster the baht, according to the World Tourism Organization (1998).

However, China had devalued their renminbi (RMB) in January 1994 that meant that they undercut prices of exports from much of East Asia in subsequent years. That event, in turn, led to deteriorating current account balances for several Asean countries. Thailand had been borrowing short term from Japan and other easy money international markets and lending long term on many real estate ventures for several years, as had Korea and other countries. Another source of pervasive weakness throughout Asia had been the financial weakness of Japan beginning in 1991 and continuing through the 1990s and beyond.

The IMF assisted Indonesia in September 1997, and Korea in December. Hong Kong was also running deficits in their current accounts and suffered a crash of about 50 percent in its stock market in late 1997. But, they held fast to their currency peg to the U.S. dollar, and bolstered their stock market with a huge influx of government money. Japan could provide relatively little financial support to the region because of their own financial problems that accelerated after 1995.

The change in sovereignty of Hong Kong from the United Kingdom to the People's Republic of China appeared to have affected the flow of tourists to Hong Kong, both before and following the actual date of the transfer. Tourists in several countries of origin, notably Japan, were encouraged by promotional campaigns to "go before the transfer" [to Chinese sovereignty]. Japanese tourism to Hong Kong reached a sharp peak in December of 1996 and plummeted during the summer of 1997. The drop in number of tourists from Japan accounted for over four-fifths of the total drop in Hong Kong tourism for the year 1997. Fortunately for purposes of measuring causal relationships, the change in sovereignty occurred at a single point in time whereas the financial factors were slower and, with the exception of Thailand, later in developing.

Tourism-including both business and pleasure travellers-is known to be very sensitive to economic conditions. Several studies reviewed by Crouch have measured the income elasticity of demand for travel to be elastic, that is, equal to or greater than 1.0 (1994a). Kulendran found much larger income elasticities for Australian tourists, perhaps due to their location (1996). Strong demand consequently has a stimulative effect on tourism when economic conditions are strengthening but work in reverse in a downturn. However, there are many other factors that potentially have impacts on tourism. See, for example, a study by Zhang that found high crime rates to be a deterrent to tourism from several countries (1998). Structural changes also are sometimes known to have very large impacts on tourism.

METHODOLOGY

This study was based on data related to tourist arrivals in Hong Kong from Japan, Mainland China, Taiwan, Thailand, Australia, the United Kingdom, and the United States. These countries accounted for nearly 80 percent of total tourist arrivals in Hong Kong during the period studied. Consumer price data were also included from Korea and Malaysia because these neighboring countries represent good substitute tourism destinations vis-à-vis Hong Kong and they devalued their currencies during the recent Asian financial crisis. See the later section, Data and Analytical Procedures, for detailed discussion of data issues and sources of data.

The fundamental principles of the models in this paper were based on the premise that quantities demanded of a given product (in this case tourism) are a function of prices of those same products (negatively), prices of competing products (positively), and incomes of the purchasers (positively). Additional factors were used to hold constant selected structural changes, the business cycle (Wong, 1997a), and seasonality that were expected to be very strong because of the use of monthly data.

The specifications of the models used in this study were based on long-term, in part non-linear demand models that included indicator or dummy variables to measure the effects of seasonality and known structural changes. Important structural changes during this period included the transfer of sovereignty of Hong Kong from the UK to the PRC as a Special Administrative Region (SAR) and devaluations of currency in selected countries, beginning with that of the 1994 devaluation of the RMB in Mainland China. Tourism impacts were standardized among countries of different sizes by defining tourist arrivals in per capita terms. Cyclical variations were standardized by use of interest rates, and prices were standardized by use of exchange rates. The long-term nature of demand was determined by use of lagged variables in autoregressive models.

Non-linearity of the demand model was due to inclusion of interest rates in squared as well as linear terms, to normalize the business cycles. The use of non-linear terms helps to ensure that no relevant forms of the variables are omitted from the model specification. Omitting such terms when in fact they are significant would lead to biased and inconsistent parameter estimates (Pindyck and Rubinfeld, 1991).

Insignificant variables were omitted from the final models in this study to improve their efficiency. An example of this omission is the linear form of interest rates in one model that found only the squared form of this variable to be significant. The inclusion of variables that are not significantly different from zero do not lead to biased or inconsistent parameter estimates but they do result in inefficiency, according to Pindyck and Rubinfeld. In addition, the inclusion of variables that have parameters not significantly different from zero leads to reader confusion because the parameters may have unexpected signs.

The detailed specifications of these demand models, especially their non-linear and autoregressive character, were expected to reduce or eliminate the potential problem of cointegration, which violates the assumptions of traditional demand models (Kulendran 1996; Wong, 1997b). Cointegration exists when time-series data are non-stationary, in which the means and variances of such variables as income and price vary over time instead of remain constant as hypothesized in traditional demand models. Kulendran noted that autoregressive distributed lag models may solve the spurious regression problem but still retain their long-term character, whereas the use of "difference" models, which usually are prescribed to eliminate cointegration, would destroy their long-term character.

Tourism in a given area represents an export or sale of products to incoming travellers. The number of tourist arrivals in Hong Kong was used in this study as the measure of the demand for tourism services. The use of expenditures would have been preferable for some purposes because of recent shifts in per capita spending but it raises various other data problems. For example, expenditure data are not normally as reliable as tourist arrival data, in part because they usually are based on surveys rather than direct measurement. Expenditures also reflect inflation that may be difficult to measure when available prices themselves are imperfect.

Prices in this study were measured by relative consumer prices faced by tourists in the country of destination (Hong Kong) relative to prices in their country of origin and prices in competing countries that draw tourists. Since a price variable related to only tourism was not available for all countries, the total CPI for each country was used as a proxy for prices of tourism products. A true price variable would include the price of transportation as well as lodging and other purchases while holding constant the quantity and quality of products purchased.

Costs of transportation among the set of countries analyzed are expected to be important variables explaining propensities to travel among various countries, because transportation costs are usually an important element of total purchases (Covington, Thunberg, and Jauregui, 1994). Costs also are expected to increase as a function of distance as a contributing factor to travel. Distance alone as a contributing factor to travel activity has often been used in gravity models that rely heavily on distance in relation to population in explaining travel activity. For example, see Uysal and Crompton (1985).

Exchange rates entered the model as factors that affect these relative prices. They can be entered as either relative exchange rates between two countries of origin and destination or by dividing the prices in the two countries by their respective exchange rates. See a similar but modified approach by Kulendran (1996). Exchange rates in this current study were defined as those published by the International Monetary Fund which relate to a basket of rates from the five largest exporting countries in the world, three of which are included in the data set used in this study (US., UK, and Japan). Since exchange rates as published are negatively related to their value in export markets, these rates were inverted so they would be expected to be positively associated with increases in Hong Kong tourist arrivals (an export).

For example, the sharp fall in the value of the euro (from 118 to the U.S. dollar in January 1999 to 103 in June 1999) was lamented as an adverse reflection on the strength of the European economies. However, that decline was welcomed by German and French exporters because their goods were thereby priced more competitively in international markets (Pfaff, 1999).

To measure the impact of competition from competing countries drawing tourists away from Hong Kong, a variable was defined as consumer prices in Hong Kong relative to prices in a combination of competing countries. That variable combined prices for all competing countries in the data set by giving them equal weight in the denominator of a separate variable, which was similar in concept but different in form from the procedure used by Loeb (1982).

The initial format of the models was patterned after that of the classic study by Witt and Witt (1992). That study, which has been cited in many more recent studies (for example, Covington, Thunberg, and Jauregui, 1994), identified factors affecting trends in international tourism to and from the United Kingdom. A 1998 study of the Asian financial problems affecting tourists travelling to Guam conducted by Dr. Joe Ismail at Purdue University for T. J. Iverson at the University of Guam was also used as a reference. In addition, the study by Kulendran related to Australian tourism arrivals was helpful in framing the models (1996).

Multiple regression assumes that the independent variables are largely independent and the subsequent error variances are also not correlated. Preliminary models using ordinary least squares regression indicated the presence of significant multicollinearity among the financial variables of GDP, CPI, exchange rates, and interest rates. This finding was verified by the relatively high levels of variance inflation factors (VIF) found for some of these variables when used in combination, despite the use of variables converted to logs. Similarly, Durbin-Watson values indicated significant levels of serial correlation in the preliminary OLS models. For that reason, autoregressive models were fit to the data for all of the final models (except for Thailand).

An autoregressive model (SAS Autoreg) with a lagged dependent variable was used to eliminate the serial correlation. The problem was expected even though the data were deseasonalized by use of indicator variables. Lagging a variable means that the model is measuring net changes in the dependent variable from one month to the next and thereby not measuring changing tastes and preferences that take more time to be expressed. Use of this variable allows one to regard the model's results as reflecting relatively long-term rather than short-term trends, according to Maddala (1992). Because the standard Durbin-Watson (dw) test for serial correlation itself is based on a first-difference comparison, it is not valid for use in autoregressive models. The Durbin Watson "h" or "t" tests can be used to test for serial correlation in lagged autoregression models (Pindyck and Rubinfeld, 1991).

The Arch (autoregressive conditional heteroscedasticity) option in the Autoreg model of SAS was used to test for the presence of heteroscedasticity (unequal variance). It was found not to be a problem in the AR models, except for the Mainland China model. In that case, the GARCH (generalized autoregressive conditional heteroscedasticity) option was used and found to normalize the variance in the model.

GARCH is a generalized error model that assumes the errors are not independent and models the conditional error variance, thereby correcting for the unequal variance. It is a maximum likelihood method with "long memory" processes that use all the past squared residuals to estimate the current variance as opposed to "short memory" used by the basic ARCH test, according to the SAS Institute's *ETS User's Guide* (1997).

The hypothesized model took the form indicated in Table 1, as an autoregressive model in log form. The log-linear form of the data was tested in early stages of model development and found to provide the best fit to the data. It is also the most common form of tourism models used in the literature, according to Crouch (1994b). The log form of the model is very convenient to use because the coefficients represent elasticities with respect to the dependent variables, but that feature alone is no justification for use of this format. The real issue to resolve is whether the elasticities in fact are constant or variable over the dataset.

Monthly data were used in the models to give sufficient data points for analysis after the onset of the financial crisis in the last quarter of 1997 and the change in sovereignty that occurred in July 1997. An additional reason for using monthly data is the need for sufficient degrees of freedom and the desirability to keep the overall length of time studied as short as possible. Keeping the time period short is important because of the dynamics of the industry and the many policy and structural changes affecting tourism in both Hong Kong and the PRC. These include shifts in visa requirements, liberalization of entry restrictions, currency importation limitations, the change in sovereignty, and avoidance of the effects of the Tiananmen Square episode.

Historical data from January 1990 through December 1998 were used as the basis for this study, to the extent that such data were avail-

TABLE 1. Hypothesized Autoregressive Model of Factors Affecting Tourist Arrivals from Six Major Countries of Origin to the Destination Country, Hong Kong

Model: $\ln T_{ijt}/P_{it} = a_1 + a_2 \ln T_{ijt}/P_{it-1} + a_3 \ln Y_{it}/P_{it} + a_4 \ln CPI_{jit} + a_5 \ln CPIS_{ji\,11}$

$+ a_6 \ln EX_{jit} + a_7 EXS_{ji\,1t} + a_8 \ln INT_{ijt} + a_9 \ln WAG_{ijt} + a_{10} \ln C_{ijt} + a_{11} \ln CS_{ijk}$

$+ a_{12} SOV + \text{Dummies} + V_{ijt}$

and $V_{ijt} = -\varphi_1 V_{ijt\,1} - \varphi_2 V_{ijt\,2} - \ldots - \varphi_{12} V_{ijt\,12} + e_{ijt}$

    $i = 1\ldots 6$ countries of origin
    $j =$ country of destination, Hong Kong
    $t = 1\ldots 108^{th}$ month (1 = Jan 1990 .... 96 = Dec 1998)

where:

T_{ijt} is the number of tourist arrivals from origin i to destination j in month t.

$T_{ijt}-1$ is a one-period, lagged dependent variable over time t.

P_{it} is the origin i population in month t.

Y_{it} is personal disposable income in origin i in time t (constant prices).

CPI_{jit} is the consumer price index in Hong Kong (j) relative to that in origin i, in month t (constant prices).

$CPIS_{ji-1t}$ is a weighted average of the consumer price index for tourists in Hong Kong (j) relative to that in i-1 substitute destinations for residents of origin i in month t (constant prices).

Ex_{jit} is the rate of exchange between currencies of Hong Kong (j) relative to that of origin i in month t; both rates are defined in terms of their relation to currencies in a basket of the five major exporting countries.

$Ex_{jj\,1t}$ is the rate of exchange between currencies in Hong Kong (j), relative to a weighted average of currencies in the remaining i − I substitute countries of origin, in month t; all rates are defined relative to rates in a basket of five major countries.

TABLE 1 (continued)

C_{ijt} is the cost of travel from origin i to Hong Kong (j) in month t (constant prices).

CIS_{ijk} is the cost of travel to substitute destinations from origin i in month t (constant prices).

INT_{ijt} is the short term interest rate (either treasury bills or money market rate) in Hong Kong (j) relative to that in the country of origin i in month t.

WAG_{ijt} is the average wage rate for all manufacturing employees in Hong Kong (j) relative to that in the country of origin i in month t (constant prices).

DEVAL is a dummy variable which measures the effect of time after devaluation of currency: (1) for PRC in January 1994 (1's), relative to the time prior to the devaluation (0's), and (2) for Thailand in July 1997 (1's), relative to the time prior to the devaluation (0's).

SOV is an indicator variable which measures the effect of the time after transfer of sovereignty of Hong Kong to PRC (1's), relative to the time prior to the transfer (0's).

D1 to D11 are indicator variables which measure the effects of monthly seasonality for January-November (1) in relation to the reference month, December (0).

e_{ijt} is the random disturbance term.

a_ks (where $k = 1,2 \ldots 23$) are unknown parameters that need to be estimated.

$\varphi_1 \ldots \varphi_{12}$ are the autoregressive error model parameters.
In denotes use of natural logarithms.

able. Gross Domestic Product (GDP) was used in place of disposable income because GDP is more comprehensive and there is a high correlation between the two. Some data, such as that for GDP, usually are available only quarterly and some data were available only annually, such as that for population for most countries. But, it was considered important to have as much detailed information available for analysis as possible, so monthly rather than quarterly data were used.

CPI data were available in index form only annually for Mainland China. But, monthly data in terms of percentage changes from the same month the year previous were also available. These data were merged into an estimate of monthly price changes in index form, by assuming that average monthly price changes over the 9-year period reflect monthly price seasonality.

Various statistical models were employed in conducting this analysis, using SAS for Windows (1997). Proc Reg and Proc Autoreg were the primary models used. The SAS program Proc Expand was used for spreading data to a common time dimension and for interpolating some missing data. Proc Expand makes use of cubic spline calculations and adjusts for differing days in a month or quarter. Use of this efficient procedure was very helpful in preserving degrees of freedom in the model. Without some procedure for allocation of monthly data, SAS could not have been used because SAS omits complete observations for all variables for which any of the variables' observations are missing. This procedure was used only when necessary to avoid unduly affecting the results.

A common data source was used whenever possible to minimize differences in definitions of data. Tourist arrival data were obtained primarily from the Hong Kong Tourist Association (1991-1998), and their personal assistance in interpreting trends in the data is recognized. Data trends were also obtained from the World Tourism Organization (1998). International Financial Statistics (1991-99) was the primary source of the financial data used.

Short-term interest rates were included to reflect the current status in time t within the business cycle. This variable was expected to be particularly relevant during the rapid changes in the economic situation accompanying the recent Asian financial crisis. Wong (1997) showed the relevance of the business cycle on tourism, and that this relationship was complex in form. For this reason, a quadratic form of the log variable was used. Interest rates are expected to be negatively associated with tourist arrivals in Hong Kong in linear form, but positive in squared form.

Wage rate data were intended as a refinement upon GDP data and a proxy for disposable income. Wage rates were hypothesized to be used either alone or in combination with GDP if collinearity problems would allow.

Transportation cost data were not available for analysis in this study so those costs were omitted from the model as fitted to the data. With the onset of yield management systems in determining prices of transportation, costs of travel likely have become less directly related to travel activity than previously, so the omission is not expected to be important. Moreover, in those studies where a relative transport cost variable was incorporated, very often insignificant statistical results were obtained; for example, see the results from Gray (1966), Little (1980), and Ismail and Iverson (1998).

FINDINGS

Table 2 contains a summary of the findings from the demand models for each of the seven countries of origin of tourist arrivals into Hong Kong. The variables are defined the same as those in Table 1, except for $LnGDP_{ijt}$ which was defined as the log of Gross Domestic Product (GDP) in all countries (j) of origin (i) in time (t), in constant dollars. The data represent the parameters of the variables in the seven models and since they are measured in logs, they represent elasticities with respect to the dependent variable, except for the indicator variables that are in nominal terms.

The models all fit the data reasonably well, with total R^2 ranging between 0.727 for the Taiwan model to 0.931 for Mainland China's model. The R^2's are totals in the sense that they included the simultaneous impacts of the autoregressive terms. Australia's model was unique in having an autoregressive term related to its residuals but did not include a significant lagged dependent variable. Thailand's model was unique in using ordinary least squares rather than an autoregressive model. In both of these models the regular Durbin-Watson statistic was measured. GDP was used as the sole indicator of level of income; wage rates had been expected to be a useful substitute for GDP in some countries, such as the PRC, but they were not significant in any model so they were omitted entirely in the final models.

Some hypothesized variables were not found to be significant in individual models and therefore were omitted from those particular models. As noted earlier, omitting those variables whose parameters were found to be insignificant increases the efficiency of the model (Pindyck and Rubinfeld, 1991). In addition, any parameter with a "t" value less than one adds nothing to the explanatory power of the model. Insignificant parameters also tend to confuse nontechnical readers because they often have intuitively incorrect signs, which would be expected when correlations are close to zero.

TABLE 2. Summary Statistics from Autoregressive Models Explaining Tourist Arrivals to Hong Kong, 1990-1998 (data are the model parameters)

Variables	Australia	Mainland China	Japan	Taiwan	Thailand	United Kingdom	United States
Intercept	−6.8397***	−0.4520**	0.1477***	2.9003***	1.0743	3.8984	18.0080***
$LnT_{ijt} - 1$		0.5379***	0.6660***	0.5035***	0.4702***	0.5877***	0.6497***
$LnGDP_{ijt}$	2.2389***	1.0139***		0.3510***			0.5575**
$LnCPI_{ijt}$	0.3431**						
$LnEX_{ijt}$							9.9570***
$LnCPI_{ijt}/lnEX_{ijt}$		−0.2458***			−0.2715 (p = 0.12)	−0.2304**	
$LnCPIS_{ij-1t}$					0.7096**	0.8865***	
$LnINT_{ijt}$		0.0398***	0.0628***	−0.0554**			
Ln^2INT_{ijt}	0.2003***						
DEVAL					−0.5759***		
SOV	0.2003***	0.1709***	−0.2985***	0.0527*		−0.1023***	−0.0372**
January		0.2260***	−0.3187***	−0.1958***	−0.7042***	0.1123**	
February	0.3305***	−0.3347***	−0.3553***	−0.1186***	−0.6942***	0.2419***	−.1326***
March			−0.1265***	0.1356***	−0.3089***	0.4657***	0.3083***
April		−0.1706***	−0.3712***			0.1583***	0.1005***
May	−0.110**		−0.2200***	−0.1456***	−0.5056***		
June		0.1865***	−0.1238**	0.1728***	−0.7690***		
July	−0.0893*	0.0808***	−0.2245***		−0.4242***	0.1757***	0.0772**
August	0.2150***	0.0907***	−0.1220***		−0.5351***	0.1765***	−0.0675*
September	0.0949**	0.1060***	−0.1629***	−0.2189***	−0.4916***	0.1854***	0.0803*
October	0.0954**	−0.0854***	−0.2519***			0.5081***	0.3801***
November	−.0930**	−0.0698***	−0.1588***	−0.2074	−0.6206***	0.2432***	
φ_1		0.2186**				0.3227	0.4453***
φ_2		0.1257*					
φ_3							
φ_4							0.2862*
φ_5	0.328***						
φ_6			0.3093***			0.2851***	
φ_7							0.2618**
φ_8				0.2883***			
φ_9							0.2468*
φ_{10}							0.2354*
φ_{12}			0.3175***				
Total R^2	0.745	0.931	0.905	0.727	0.893	0.888	0.837
Durbin h/t Prob.	1.775 (1) 0.080	0.808(t) 0.211	−1.658 (h) 0.048	−0.137 (t) 0.446	1.96 (1) 0.001	3.009 (h) 0.001	−1.143(t) 0.128

Significance levels: * indicates 10 percent, ** indicates 5 percent, and *** indicates 1 percent.

Trends in tourist arrivals were found to be very strong, as measured by the highly significant, positive lags of 0.5 or 0.6 in the dependent variables in all models except for Australia. In all cases, these variables were highly significant, which was not surprising in view of the monthly data analyzed.

GDP in real terms is a strong variable explaining the number of tourist arrivals from Australia, Mainland China, Taiwan, and the United States. For Australia and Mainland China, the large coefficient (elasticities) of more than 1.0 in logs implies that a 1-percent increase (or decrease) in real GDP in these countries of origin resulted in more than a 1-percent increase (or decrease) in number of tourists going to Hong Kong. These are large impacts that are positive in good economic times but strongly negative when incomes decline. Therefore, the strong economic growth in both Mainland China and Australia work strongly to the advantage of tourism in Hong Kong. The findings for Australia confirm the results of past studies cited by Crouch which found long-haul destinations to be more income sensitive and less price sensitive than short-haul destinations (1994a). The U.S. and Taiwan coefficients of 0.55 and 0.35, respectively, although inelastic at less than 1.0, also demonstrate that Hong Kong tourism benefited importantly from the strong economies in these countries during the decade of the 1990s.

The models varied in terms of how the consumer price index and exchange rates entered the model. In the UK, Mainland China, and Thailand (significant at 0.12 level) models, prices entered as a ratio of the relative CPIs divided by a ratio of the relative exchange rates. For the US model, only exchange rates alone entered the model, and in the Australian model, consumer prices alone entered the model. The coefficients for relative consumer prices (alone) are negative and for exchange rates (alone) were positive, as expected. The U.S. model contains a very large coefficient for exchange rates because the changes in exchange rates relative to the 5-country benchmark are very small owing to the Hong Kong dollar being pegged to the U.S. dollar.

When relative consumer prices were deflated by relative exchange rates, the coefficients were also negative, as expected. The price parameters (elasticities) relative to exchange rates for Mainland China, UK, and Thailand were all about the same level of magnitude, and were especially significant for Mainland China. This consistency is encouraging, particularly for Mainland China which still has some restrictions to free travel.

For two countries, Thailand and the UK, sizeable and positive coefficients (elasticities of 0.71 and 0.89) were found on relative consumer prices in competing countries of destination. This variable represents a cross-elasticity of demand for tourism, which indicates that as prices rise in competing countries of destination relative to Hong Kong's prices, Hong Kong tourist arrivals increase almost proportionately.

In addition, the Thailand model shows that tourism to Hong Kong was reduced sharply after July 1997, over and above the effects of other variables in the model. Thailand devalued its currency at that time which was the same time period as the change in sovereignty in Hong Kong. In Thailand's case, the simultaneity of the financial crisis with the change in sovereignty makes it difficult to assess the cause of the decline. Thus, this effect is attributed to a devaluation (DEVAL) variable in the model that includes the effects of the change in sovereignty. A DEVAL variable was also included in the Mainland China model, but it was not significant and therefore dropped from the final model.

Four countries, Australia, Mainland China, Japan, and Taiwan showed that changes in interest rates in the country of origin relative to Hong Kong affected tourism flows to Hong Kong; this variable is regarded as a proxy for changes in the business cycle. For Taiwan the effects were negative, as expected, which indicates that tourism to Hong Kong increased when interest rates at home declined, and the economy is improving. But for Japan and Mainland China, the impacts were positive, which indicates that rising interest rates at home were associated with increasing tourist arrivals in Hong Kong, which seems counterintuitive. For the Australian model, the interest rate variable was in quadratic form, positive and highly significant, indicating its strong impact.

For Japan, neither relative consumer prices nor exchange rates entered the model. The non-economic variables were found to be stronger than the economic variables. The single exception was interest rates in Japan that moved positively with number of tourist arrivals in Hong Kong, perhaps as a result of the extremely low interest rates in Japan in recent years. GDP was not a significant variable in this model, even in the absence of other economic variables. These comparisons suggest that relative interest rates, trends in tourism, the change in sovereignty, and seasonality accounted for much of the sharp decline in number of Japanese tourists travelling to Hong Kong. The poor economic situation in Japan is a factor, expressed more strongly in relative interest rates than in relative consumer prices, but neither one appears to be a strong factor in the strong decline in tourism from Japan in recent years. These findings gives no support to the idea that the July 1997 decline in tourism was temporary or due to discriminatory hotel prices at that time, as some surveys have suggested. Apparently, much of the Japanese travel to Hong Kong is discretionary rather than business related, according to Heung and Qu (1999).

The variable for the July 1997 change in sovereignty of Hong Kong to that of becoming a Special Administrative Region (SAR) of the PRC was highly significant for all models (Thailand was indeterminate). This variable was the strongest for Japan, Australia and Mainland China and the weakest for Taiwan, the U.S. and the UK. The finding for the UK is perhaps surprising in view of their loss of Hong Kong to the PRC. The UK continues to travel there at a relatively high rate whereas the rate of Japanese travel dropped sharply in May-July 1997 and apparently has not recovered.

Seasonality was found to be very important for explaining tourist arrivals in Hong Kong; it was relatively the strongest for Japanese travellers. Each month of the year for that model contained a significant seasonal coefficient. The reference year in all models was December which was at or near the seasonal peak for all the Asian countries although it is the seasonal low-point for the UK. This conclusion is supported by the negative signs on all coefficients for Japan, China, Taiwan and Thailand and positive signs on all of the coefficients for the UK. Australia joins the Asian countries in having most month's seasonal factors lower than in December, and the U.S. joins the UK in having most month's factors higher than in December.

CONCLUSIONS

The study identified variables that explain upwards of nine-tenths of the total variation in a set of models explaining levels of tourist arrivals in Hong Kong. Financial variables such as gross domestic product, relative prices, exchange rates, and interest rates were found to be very important in determining the level of tourist arrivals in Hong Kong.

The level of Gross Domestic Product in real terms was found to be the most important financial variable, particularly in the case of Australia and Mainland China which increased their rates of increase in number of travellers at one to two times the rates of their increases in GDP. Declines in real levels of GDP or even moderating increases during the Asian crisis obviously had strong adverse impacts on Hong Kong tourism.

Relative consumer price levels between Hong Kong and the countries of origin, either alone or adjusted by relative exchange rates, were also found to be important influences in explaining tourist flows among most of the countries studied. The impacts on number of tourists were found to be in the range of -0.2 to -0.3 percent for every 1-percent increase in relative CPI in Hong Kong relative to the major countries of origin. The very dramatic adverse changes in exchange rates due to the financial crisis working its way around the region obviously had dramatic impacts on relative real consumer prices. Part of these impacts were expressed in terms of rapidly changing airline fares which were not specifically included in this study.

Japan was the major exception to these trends; their tourists were more dependent on trends and structural variables than on economic variables. Perhaps this finding reflects their tendency to travel in groups, and to be largely composed of relatively young, pleasure travellers. This finding for Japan-which is the country of origin that has declined the most in tourist arrivals to Hong Kong-does not support the hypothesis that Japanese tourist arrivals have declined as a result of their perception of high prices of tourism products in Hong Kong. The Japanese apparently declined to vacation in Hong Kong after the change in sovereignty for personal rather than economic reasons, perhaps due to the influence of their many tourist guides.

The change in sovereignty of Hong Kong in July 1997 was associated with substantial declines in tourism to Hong Kong from other countries as well as Japan, after allowing for other variables. Taiwan has been the least strongly affected. The declines due to the change in sovereignty were strong even from Mainland China, after allowing for financial, seasonal, and other factors. The sovereignty impact may soften as time passes but had not done so by the end of the study period, December 1998.

Finally, seasonality was found to have a very important impact on the rate of tourist arrivals from various source countries. Most months experienced changes of 200-300 (reflecting coefficients of 0.2 to 0.3) per month for individual countries, after the effects of other factors. These seasonal factors differed substantially among different countries of origin and their effects were offsetting to a large degree. The Asian countries' tourist arrivals tended to peak late in the year, (December) whereas the western countries' arrivals tended to peak during the spring (March) and fall (October).

To measure the effects of the Asian financial crisis on Hong Kong tourism from a particular country, one can take the financial coefficients of that country (or a closely related country) and apply them to the changes in the respective financial parameters of that country. Similarly, projections of tourist arrivals can be made using these parameters, but first one needs to obtain good projections of the key variables like GDP, consumer prices, and exchange rates.

LIMITATIONS AND FUTURE RESEARCH

There are several opportunities for further research that could improve or extend the findings of this study. These include improvements in prices related to tourism, development of models explaining tourism expenditures, and development of cointegration models.

Prices of tourism are difficult concepts to measure in the case of international tourism. Available prices include prices for all consumer items when one would prefer to have prices related specifically to the purchase of tourism products such as airline tickets and lodging services that are much more important for travellers than for other consumers. Price inflation can have strange impacts when price relationship change for tourism relative to general consumer products. The consumer price variables in the current models would be much stronger if prices for transportation services and lodging services could have been incorporated in a total price index for tourism goods and services. Similarly, cross-price elasticities of demand among substitute destinations were found to be meaningful in only two models analyzed in this study. More precise price data likely would show these variables to be much stronger in the other models.

Using expenditures as the measure of demand rather than tourist arrivals would add a useful follow-up study to see if this measure supported or conflicted with the current study. This approach would be particularly helpful in explaining variations in demand associated with length of stay and varying levels of per capita spending among tourists from alternative countries. But, expenditures as a measure of demand suffers its own shortcomings so it is not used as often as tourist arrivals in measuring demand. The main problem is that it confounds the measurement of both prices and quantity, because expenditures are a combination of the two together. Dividing expenditures by prices to derive quantities depends importantly on having appropriate prices, and not changing the quality or mix of products being purchased over the period of study. Most expenditure data are based on sample surveys rather than enumeration, which adds sampling variability to the problem of getting accurate data.

Another useful study would be to change the specifications of the models to pattern the error correction and cointegration modeling techniques that have gained acceptance in demand studies in recent years. There appears to be little question but that the OLS models used traditionally were dealing with data that often were non-stationary. These approaches would substitute for the autoregressive and non-linear techniques used in this study that have attempted to measure the real world.

Finally, the time period since the change in sovereignty had been quite short prior to the end of the study period. But, the financial factors affecting the region have remained in flux. Many countries have recovered economically, but not Japan. Therefore, it may be useful to replicate these tourism demand models in a few years to test their dynamic properties.

REFERENCES

Covington, B., Thunberg, E. M. & Jauregui, C. (1994). International demand for the United States as a travel destination. *Journal of Travel and Tourism Marketing*, 3(4), 39-50.

Crouch, G. I. (1994a). The study of international tourism demand: A review of findings. *Journal of Travel Research*, 33 (1), 12-23.

Crouch, G. I. (1994b). The study of international tourism demand: A survey of practice. *Journal of Travel Research*, 32 (4), 41-57.

Crouch, G. I. (1994c). Guidelines for the study of international tourism demand using regression analysis. Chapter 51 in *Travel, Tourism, and Hospitality Research: A Handbook for Managers and Researchers*. (2nd edition). Eds. J. R. B. Ritche and C. R. Goeldner. New York: John Wiley & Sons, pp. 583-596.

Gray, H. P. (1966). The demand for international travel by the United States and Canada. *International Economic Review*, 7, 83-92.

Heung, C. S. & Qu. H. (2000). Hong Kong as a travel destination: An analysis of Japanese tourists' satisfaction levels, and the likelihood of them recommending Hong Kong to others. *Journal of Travel and Tourism Marketing*, 9 (1/2).

Hong Kong Tourist Association (1991-1998). *A Statistical Review of Tourism* (1990-1998 editions). Hong Kong: P.O. Box 2597 G.P.O.

Ismail, J. A. & Iverson, T. J. (1998). *Econometric Modeling of Japanese Visitors to Guam. Research.* report submitted to the University of Guam, Mangilao, Guam.

International Monetary Fund (1991-99) *International Financial Statistics*. Electronic edn.

Kulendran, N. (1996). Modelling quarterly tourist flows to Australia using cointegration analysis. *Tourism Economics*, 2 (3), 203-222.

Little, J.S. (1980). 1980 International Travel in the U.S. Balance of Payments. *New England Economic Review*, May/June, 42-55.

Loeb, P. D. (1982). International travel to the United States: An econometric evaluation. *Annals of Tourism Research*, 9 (1), 7-20.

Maddala, G. S. (1992). *Introduction to Econometrics* (12th edition). New York: Macmillan.

Pindyck, R. S. & Rubinfeld, D. L. (1991) *Econometric Models* (3rd edition). New York: McGraw-Hill, Inc.

Pfaff, W. (1999). The bright side of the euro's weakness. *International Herald Tribune*. Hong Kong, June 3.

Plog Research, Inc. (1997). Views about Hong Kong: report on a four country study of the reasons for the post-handover tourism decline, report prepared for the Hong Kong Tourist Association, No. 26-3481, Hong Kong.

SAS Institute, Inc. (1997). *SAS/ETS User's Guide*, SAS v. 7 Online Documentation. Cary, North Carolina.

Uysal, M. & Crompton, J. (1985). An overview of approaches used to forecast tourism demand. *Journal of Travel Research*, 42(4), 7-15.

World Tourism Organization, Commission for East Asia and the Pacific (1998). *Tourism Market Trends: East Asia and the Pacific*, 1988-1997, 32nd meeting, Kyoto, Japan. Madrid: World Tourism Organization.

Witt, S. & Witt, W. (1992). *Modeling and Forecasting Demand in Tourism*. London: Academic Press, Harcourt Brace Jovanovich.

Wong, K. F. (1997a). The relevance of business cycles in forecasting international tourist arrivals. *Tourism Management*, 18 (8), 581-586.

Wong, K. F. (1997b). An investigation of the integrated properties of a time series data: international tourist arrivals. Paper presented at the 1997 conference of the Asia Pacific Tourism Association, 3(2), 185-199.

Zhang, H. Q. (1998). The importance of income, the exchange rate, and the crime rate in influencing demand for Hong Kong as an international tourist destination. *Australian Journal of Hospitality Management*, 5 (1), 1-7. The University of Queensland.

Modeling Tourist Flows
to Indonesia and Malaysia

Amy Y. F. Tan
Cynthia McCahon
Judy Miller

SUMMARY. The purpose of this study was to examine the major factors that influence the flow patterns of tourists from six important tourist-generating countries to Indonesia and Malaysia. The primary determinants included in the demand models were income, prices, and time trend. Two models that employed different indicators for the price variable were estimated; one with exchange rates in addition to relative prices, whereas the other included only an exchange rate adjusted-relative price variable. Annual time-series data covering the period 1980 to 1997 were used for estimation. The results generally indicated that the factors provide reasonably good explanations for the demand for Indonesian and Malaysian tourism. The measure of the joint effect of the changes in exchange rates and relative prices also seems to be a better indicator for the price variable for both destination countries. The study

Amy Y. F. Tan is Assistant Professor in the School of Hotel and Tourism Management, The Hong Kong Polytechnic University. Cynthia McCahon is Associate Professor in the College of Business Administration, Kansas State University and Judy Miller is Emeritus Professor in the Hotel, Restaurant, and Institutional Management and Dietetics Department, Kansas State University.

Address correspondence to: Amy Y. F. Tan, School of Hotel and Tourism Management, The Hong Kong Polytechnic University, Hung Hum, Kowloon, Hong Kong SAR (E-mail: hmamy@polyu.edu.hk).

[Haworth co-indexing entry note]: "Modeling Tourist Flows to Indonesia and Malaysia." Tan, Amy Y. F., Cynthia McCahon, and Judy Miller. Co-published simultaneously in *Journal of Travel & Tourism Marketing* (The Haworth Hospitality Press, an imprint of The Haworth Press, Inc.) Vol. 13, No. 1/2, 2002, pp. 63-84; and: *Tourism Forecasting and Marketing* (ed: Kevin K. F. Wong and Haiyan Song) The Haworth Hospitality Press, an imprint of The Haworth Press, Inc., 2002, pp. 63-84. Single or multiple copies of this article are available for a fee from The Haworth Document Delivery Service [1-800-HAWORTH, 9:00 a.m. - 5:00 p.m. (EST). E-mail address: getinfo@haworthpressinc.com].

has important marketing implications for the tourism industries in Indonesia and Malaysia. *[Article copies available for a fee from The Haworth Document Delivery Service: 1-800-HAWORTH. E-mail address: <getinfo@haworthpressinc.com> Website: <http://www.HaworthPress.com> © 2002 by The Haworth Press, Inc. All rights reserved.]*

KEYWORDS. Tourism demand, demand elasticity, econometric model

INTRODUCTION

The rapid growth of international tourism over the past three decades has attracted considerable attention in many developing nations, including Indonesia and Malaysia. The growing importance of tourism in these countries is indicated by their tourism revenues for the past 17 years. They rose from an estimated $246 million in 1980 to $6.6 billion in 1997, an approximate 26-fold increase, for Indonesia, and increased 11-fold, from $317 million in 1980 to $3.9 billion in 1997, for Malaysia (United Nations Statistical Yearbook, 1985; World Tourism Organization, 1998). Because of these increases, the tourism industry has since been included as an integral part in the economic planning of Indonesia and Malaysia.

Among all destinations in Southeast Asia, Indonesia and Malaysia are the most similar in terms of their geographical location, people, history, language, culture, and natural resources. The two nations also sell the same attractions: beaches, mountains, cultural diversity, performing arts and handicrafts (Aznam, 1992). Most importantly, the governments of both nations only began to emphasize the tourism sector in the early 1980s (Liden and Tyler, 1992; Schwarz, 1988). Being late comers into the tourism industry, Indonesia and Malaysia face a great deal of competition to obtain a share of this market. In view of the fierce competition and the many opportunities presented by the tourism industry, factors that affect international tourists' demand for Indonesia and Malaysia deserve immediate attention. Also, identification of the underlying causes for tourist flow patterns is important for efficient planning and management of inbound tourism in the countries.

The econometric approach has been one of the most popular techniques for studying the determinants of international tourism demand. This is because the theoretical framework for this type of study rests heavily upon the principles of demand in economics. However, previ-

ous studies using econometric modeling of tourist demand have focused mainly on the developed nations and have not considered this
aspect of tourism in Indonesia and Malaysia. Hence, the purpose of this
study was to examine the major economic factors that influence the
flow patterns of tourists to Indonesia and Malaysia using the econometric approach.

INBOUND TOURISM DEMAND IN INDONESIA AND MALAYSIA

Figure 1 presents the total tourist arrivals for Indonesia and Malaysia
from 1981 to 1997. The number of tourist arrivals in Indonesia grew approximately eightfold, from 600,000 in 1981 to about 5 million in 1997,
at an average annual rate of 14.8 percent. Tourist arrivals to Malaysia,
on the other hand, increased from 1.6 million to 6.2 million from 1981
to 1997, at an average annual rate of 9.5 percent.

Several important events in the 17 years have been noted for their influences on tourist flow patterns in Indonesia and Malaysia. The huge
surges of tourists in Malaysia in 1990 and 1994 were attributed to its
"Visit Malaysia Year" campaigns (Anonymous, 1993b; Anonymous,
1997b; King, 1994). The substantial effort of the "Visit ASEAN (Association of Southeast Asian Nations) Year 1992" campaign, which was

FIGURE 1. Tourist Arrivals in Indonesia and Malaysia

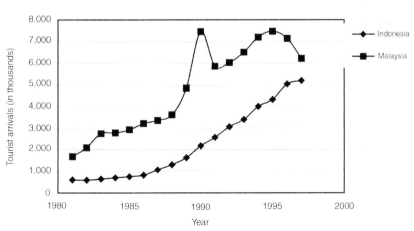

directed at the ASEAN nations themselves (Brunei Darusallam, Indonesia, Malaysia, Philippines, Singapore, and Thailand) as well as the Australian, German, and Japanese markets, was credited for the increases in tourist arrivals to Indonesia and Malaysia in 1992 (Anonymous, 1993a; Schansman, 1991). On the other hand, the negative impact of the Gulf War has been speculated often as the main reason for the slower growth in the number of visits in Indonesia (from 34 percent in 1990 to 18 percent in 1991) (Mcbeth, 1994; Schansman, 1991) and the drastic drop in tourists for Malaysia in 1991 (from 54 percent in 1990 to -22 percent in 1991) (Goldsmith and Zahari, 1994; Mohamed, 1995; Selwitz, 1991; Soledad, 1996). In 1997, the tourist industry in Indonesia experienced its first stagnant period in the decade, whereas that in Malaysia experienced a negative growth. This bad performance was attributed to the Asian currency crisis and the outbreaks of forest fires in Indonesia (Leiper and Hing, 1998).

The biggest tourist supplier for Indonesia and Malaysia is the Asian Pacific region. Between 1985 to 1997, this region alone contributed an average of 71 percent and 87 percent of tourist arrivals to Indonesia and Malaysia, respectively (World Tourism Organization, 1998). Among all countries in Asia, Singapore and Japan have emerged as two of the most important suppliers of tourists to both countries. Together with the United Kingdom (UK), Germany, Australia, and the United States of America (USA), they contributed over 50 percent of Indonesia's and Malaysia's tourists between 1985 to 1997 (World Tourism Organization, 1998). With the recent decline in regional international travel as a result of the Asian economic downturn, long-haul markets such as the USA, UK, and Germany have grown to become more important for both destinations. These tourist-generating countries are more likely to be the primary sources of supply of "hard" currencies for reforming the Indonesian and Malaysian economies in the near future.

DETERMINANTS OF INTERNATIONAL TOURISM DEMAND

A review of past literature revealed a wide array of factors that affect international vacation demand. Income usually has been cited as the most important variable that provided the greatest explanatory power (Akis, 1998; Anastasopoulos, 1989; Covington et al., 1994; Crouch et al., 1992; Hui and Yuen, 1996; Jud and Joseph, 1974; Kwack, 1972; Lee, 1996; Loeb, 1982; Qu and Lam, 1997; Uysal and Crompton, 1984; Webber, 2001), although it occasionally has been found to be insignificant in influencing tourist demand for certain countries (Crouch, 2000; Dritsakis & Athanasiadis, 2000; Vogt and Wittayakorn, 1998). Following the basic principle of demand in economics, the demand for a travel destination country is expected to surge with an increase in the tourist-generating country's income, holding all other factors constant. Private consumption or personal disposable income has been suggested as the best measure for vacation visits, but gross national product (GNP) and gross domestic product (GDP) also were used frequently in vacation demand functions (Di Matteo and Di Matteo, 1993; Hui and Yuen, 1996; Jud and Joseph, 1974; Lee, 1996; Uysal and Crompton, 1984). Empirical results of past tourism demand models often have been viewed in terms of elasticity of demand. The estimated income elasticities commonly were found to be positive and above unity (greater than 1), albeit a negative income elasticity, which denoted inferior tourism destinations, was observed occasionally (Chadee and Mieczkowski, 1987).

Price is another important factor that has appeared frequently in the travel demand functions as: (1) the prices of tourist goods and services in the destination country; (2) the effect of exchange rate changes on purchasing power; and (3) the transportation costs between countries (Crouch, 1994b; O'Hagan and Harrison, 1984; Witt and Witt, 1992).

Basic economic demand theory implies that the higher the prices of tourist goods and services at a destination, the lower the tourism demand, other things remaining constant. However, tourists' demand for a particular travel destination also may be a response to changes in the prices of other alternative destinations or domestic tourism in the origin country. Hence, the destination price variable in typical travel demand models frequently has been specified in relative form to account for the cross-price effect. In the past, use of a tourist price index or other similar indices defined over all goods purchased by tourists, has been suggested as the best form of measurement. However, such data often are not available for most countries. The consumer price index (CPI) has been used instead as a proxy measure in most studies (Akis, 1998; Crouch et al., 1992; Lathiras and Siriopoulos, 1998; Lee, 1996; Rosensweig, 1986; Stronge and Redman, 1982; Qu and Lam, 1997; Uysal and Crompton, 1984). Martin and Witt (1987) who compared the explanatory power of a tourist price index and the CPI, concluded that there is no evidence of clear superiority of the former variable, but the CPI is a reasonable proxy for the cost of tourism. The results of Morley (1994) further confirmed the use of CPI as a proxy for tourism prices in demand models. The findings for the effect of destination prices upon foreign travel demand have varied widely. The variable was significant in many cases, but several studies found an unexpected positive sign and/or statistically insignificant values (Crouch, 1994b; Jud and Joseph, 1974; Kwack, 1972; Little, 1980; Loeb, 1982; Martin and Witt, 1988; Qu and Lam, 1997; Uysal and Crompton, 1984).

The relationship between changes in a country's price levels and the changes in its currency values remains a complicated and unresolved issue for modeling tourism demand functions (Gray, 1966). In the past, the effect of exchange rate changes often was accounted for indirectly by converting the destination price variable (either a tourist price index or an equivalent measure such as the CPI) into the currency of the tourist-generating country (Jud and Joseph, 1974; Kliman, 1981). However, the recent practice has been to model exchange rate as a separate explanatory variable in addition to the destination price variable. It is believed that the rapid changes in exchange rates are perceived more readily by potential foreign travelers than changes in the country's price levels (Gray, 1966; O'Hagan and Harrison, 1984; Witt and Witt, 1992). When the exchange rate is included as a separate independent variable in a travel demand function, the depreciation of a destination's currency relative to an origin country's currency is expected to lead to an increase in international tourism demand for the destination. This hypothesis has been supported by certain studies (Gerakis, 1965; Hui and Yuen, 1996; Lin and Sung, 1983; Rosensweig, 1986; Webber, 2001) but not by others (Chadee and Mieczkowski, 1987; Dritsakis and Athanasiadis, 2000; Gray, 1966; Loeb, 1982; Qu and Lam, 1997; Summary, 1987).

An increase in travel costs is expected to result in a decline in international travel, holding other factors constant. Previous studies that attempted to examine travel cost as a determinant for tourism flows were concerned mainly about the costs of travel by air between origin and destination major cities. Results regarding the impact of travel cost upon tourism demand are very uncertain. The variable was found to be significant in some studies (Covington et al., 1994; Jud and Joseph, 1974; Kliman, 1981) and insignificant in others (Gray, 1966; Little, 1980).

The demand for vacation destinations also may be subject to changes in the popularity of the destination over time as a result of changing consumer preferences. Hence, some of the past studies have attempted to account for this factor by incorporating a time-trend in the demand function. In addition to capturing the effect of changing consumer tastes for a specific travel destination, the time-trend factor also accounts for all time effects of other explanatory variables not explicitly included in the demand function (Witt and Witt, 1992). Demand theory implies that the estimated coefficient of the trend term can be either positive or negative, depending on the degree of the popularity of the destination over time. However, the effect of the trend factor in previous tourism demand studies has not been consistent. For instance, Crouch et al. (1992) found the variable to have little measurable effect on international travel demand for Australia, while other conclusions varied from weak to moderately strong (Crouch, 1994b; Crouch, 2000).

Demand for a vacation destination also may be affected by special events. A variety of these, such as political instability, social conflict, terrorism, economic recessions, world fairs, and sports, have been modeled through dummy variables (Crouch, 1994a; Di Matteo and Di Matteo, 1993; Rosensweig, 1986; Summary, 1987; Witt and Martin, 1987). However, results for each specific event or situation varied considerably from study to study and country to country.

Other factors of particular interest in the tourism demand literature included measures of marketing effort and the dynamic structure of time-series. Although the importance of marketing expenditures by private or national agencies are vital for promoting the country as a destination, only a limited number of past studies have included the variable because of three reasons (Crouch, 1994b; Tremblay, 1989; Witt and Martin, 1987; Witt and Witt, 1992): (1) the difficulty in obtaining the relevant data; (2) the variable is being highly correlated with the income variable; and (3) the promotional effectiveness in influencing the level of international tourism demand may vary across media, which further complicates its measurement. For studies that have attempted to examine this effect, the marketing elasticities often had the expected positive sign (Crouch, 2000; Crouch et al., 1992; Dritsakis and Athanasiadis, 2000; Lee, 1996), but whether its impact was significant varied from case to case.

The inclusion of the lagged dependent variable has been the most common approach to model the dynamic effects in tourism demand functions (Lim, 1997; Morley, 1998). However, the inclusion of such variable into the demand models generally was not popular among previous researchers. Only a limited number of studies examined its impact on international tourism demand, and some ultimately removed the variable from the demand functions due to certain statistical problems such as serial correlation or multicollinearity. Morley (1998) also noted that the simple inclusion of the lagged dependent variable might not be the most appropriate way to represent dynamics of the tourism models, because the reasons for its inclusion in the past generally were not based on any rigorous theoretical framework. Recent attempts that addressed the issue of non-stationary time-series included the use of cointegration technique (Jensen, 1998; Kulendran, 1996; Song and Witt, 2000; Vogt and Wittayakorn, 1998; Webber, 2001), the error correction mechanism (Song and Witt, 2000; Lathiras and Siriopoulos, 1998), and the specification of a nonlinear, diffusion form of model (Morley, 1998).

METHODOLOGY

Model Specification

Econometric models were estimated to explain tourist flows from each of the six tourist generating-countries (Singapore, Japan, Australia, USA, UK, and Germany) to each of the two destinations (Indonesia and Malaysia). The basic demand model employed is based on the classic demand theory of economics, which suggests that demand is affected by changes in income of consumers, prices of goods and services, and preferences of consumers. A review of related literature and the availability of data were also primary sources of concern in formulating the models for this study. The major determinants of international tourism demand for Indonesia and Malaysia therefore included measures of income, relative prices, exchange rates, trend term, and special events.

Because of the complex nature of the price variable, two models that employed different indicators were used to analyze the tourist flow patterns to Indonesia and Malaysia. The first model used exchange rates in addition to the relative price variable as indicators for prices. The second model examined the hybrid effect of these variables by including merely the exchange rate-adjusted relative prices. The following models were estimated for each pair of origin-destination countries:

$$\ln (TA_{ijt}/ P_{it}) = \beta_0 + \beta_1 \ln(Income_{it}/P_{it}) + \beta_2 \ln Rprice_{ijt} + \beta_3 \ln Ex_{ijt} + \beta_4 Trend_t$$
$$+ \beta_5 D_1 + \dots + \beta_m D_n + \varepsilon \qquad \text{(Model 1)}$$

$$\ln (TA_{ijt}/ P_{it}) = \lambda_0 + \lambda_1 \ln(Income_{it}/P_{it}) + \lambda_2 \ln Exrp_{ijt} + \lambda_3 Trend_t$$
$$+ \lambda_4 D_1 + \dots + \lambda_m D_n + \varepsilon \qquad \text{(Model 2)}$$

where

TA_{ijt} Tourist arrivals from origin country i to destination country j in year t

P_{it} — Origin country i population in year t

$Income_{it}$ — GDP in origin country i in year t

$Rprice_{ijt}$ — CPI in destination country j relative to CPI in origin country i in year t

Ex_{ijt} — Currency of destination country j per unit of currency of origin country i in year t

$Trend_t$ — Time trend (defined as 1980 = 1, 1981 = 2 and so on)

$Exrp_{ijt}$ — CPI in destination country j relative to CPI in origin country i in year t (with an exchange rate adjustment)

$D_1 \ldots D_n$ — Dummy variables representing special events

ε — Random error term

β, λ — Coefficients to be estimated

The dependent variable in this study was measured as the per capita visits from the tourist generating-country to Indonesia (Malaysia). This was done to remove the effect of increases in tourist arrivals due merely to population growth.

The GDP in the origin country's currency was used to represent the income variable. Data for the GDP were defined in real per capita form to account for the effects of population growth and inflation in each origin country.

The relative price variable was measured as the CPI of the destination country relative to the CPI of the origin country in a given year. For Model 2, however, the relative CPI was converted to the origin country's currency. Hence, the final form of the relative price variable for Model 2 consists of a combination of the effects of changes in prices and exchange rates. The measure of relative prices for both models considered only domestic tourism in the origin country and the trip to Indonesia (Malaysia) as the principal choices for potential travelers. Although Witt and Martin (1987) suggested the use of a weighted average of prices for a selected set of competing destinations for the origin country under consideration, substitute destination(s) for both Indonesia and Malaysia were not readily apparent. Nevertheless, the two approaches used to operationalize the relative price variable were the most commonly found methods in previous studies (Crouch et al., 1992; Jud and Joseph, 1974; Kliman, 1981; Lee, 1996; Witt and Witt, 1992).

The exchange rate variable used in Model 1 was defined in the destination country's real currency per unit of origin country's currency.

Therefore, any significant changes in the number of visits to Indonesia and Malaysia could not be attributed to the effect of inflation.

Dummy variables also were included in the models to account for a number of special events: D_1 for the Persian Gulf War in 1991; D_2 for the Visit ASEAN Year in 1992 (applicable to Japan, Singapore, Australia, and Germany only); D_3 for the environmental and the Asia currency crises in 1997; and D_4 for the Visit Malaysia Year campaigns in 1990 and 1994. Only D_1 to D_3 were included in the models for Indonesia, whereas D_1 to D_4 were estimated in the models for Malaysia. The sign of the coefficient for D_3 could be either positive or negative, depending on whether the outbreaks of forest fires had a more dominant and sustaining effect than the exchange rate benefit gained by the origin country as a result of the Asian currency crisis or vice versa.

Models 1 and 2 thus postulate that tourist arrival per capita from each of the tourist-generating countries is a function of per capita real income, relative prices, real exchange rate, trend, and special events. It is hypothesized that:

$$\beta_1 > 0; \beta_2 < 0; \beta_3 > 0; \beta_4 < 0 \text{ or } \beta_4 > 0; \beta_5 < 0; \beta_6 > 0; \beta_7 < 0 \text{ or } \beta_7 > 0; \beta_8 > 0 \qquad \text{(Model 1)}$$

$$\lambda_1 > 0; \lambda_2 < 0; \lambda_3 < 0 \text{ or } \lambda_3 > 0; \lambda_4 < 0; \lambda_5 > 0; \lambda_6 < 0 \text{ or } \lambda_6 > 0; \lambda_7 > 0 \qquad \text{(Model 2)}$$

Because of the limited data available in Indonesia and Malaysia, a travel cost variable was not included in the demand models. Many studies in the past also did not include travel cost in the demand functions for the following reasons: (1) inconsistency and lack of data; (2) the complexity of the transportation cost structure; (3) the problem of multicollinearity between travel cost and income in the demand models (Kwack, 1972; Lee, 1996; Loeb, 1982; O'Hagan and Harrison, 1984; Uysal and Crompton, 1984). The exact consequences of omitting travel cost in a demand model remain inconclusive. However, Crouch (1996), who integrated a large number of tourism demand studies through the application of meta-analysis, concluded that the omission of the travel cost variable generally did not significantly influence the estimated income and price elasticities of demand. Other excluded explanatory variables that might explain variations in the demand for tourism in Indonesia and Malaysia were expected to be captured by the error term.

The double-log functional form of the demand equation was chosen to test the data. This model has an advantage that the resulting estimated regression coefficients in this functional form can be interpreted directly as the demand elasticities. In addition, previous researchers who have tested the suitability of different functional forms in the context of international travel demand seem to agree that the double-log form tends to provide a better fit to the data (Crouch, 1994a; Lee, 1996; Witt and Witt, 1995).

Data Sources

Annual time series data covering the period 1980 to 1997 were used for estimating each pair of origin-destination countries. The data on GDP, CPI, exchange rate, and population were obtained from the International Financial Statistics Yearbook published by the International Monetary Fund (1998). Data on tourist arrivals were obtained from the World Tourism Organization (1998), the United Nations Statistical Yearbook (1981 to 1985), the Statistical Information Services of Indonesia (Y. Supriatna, personal communication, January 30, 2000), and the Malaysian Tourism Promotion Board (N. A. Wahid, personal communication, February 21, 2000).

Data Analysis

The ordinary least square (OLS) multiple regression technique, which has dominated the estimation procedure in past tourism demand models, was utilized to estimate the demand for Indonesia and Malaysia as travel destinations. When multicollinearity was present, the problem was overcome partially by eliminating insignificant coefficients from the equation one at a time, and a number of regression runs that involved different combinations of the independent variables (those that were not strongly correlated) were undertaken.

The presence of first-order serial correlation (correlation among the residual terms) was another major concern, and it was detected by Durbin-Watson (DW) statistics. When the DW test gave inconclusive results, Saunders et al. (as cited by Witt and Witt, 1992) suggested the rule of approximation was to assume independent errors for models with DW values within the range of 1.5 to 2.5. In cases where the error terms were found to be serially dependent in the models, the Cochrane-Orcutt (CORC) iterative procedure was used as the alternative estimating method.

RESULTS

Two models that employed different measures for the relative price variable were analyzed for each pair of origin-destination countries. However, the measure of the hybrid effect of the changes in exchange rates and the relative CPI (Model 2) seemed to be a better indicator of the relative price variable for both Indonesia and Malaysia for three reasons. First, the coefficients were more consistent with the expected negative signs, and this criterion is especially important when the regression models are used for forecasting purposes (Witt and Martin, 1987). Secondly, the use of fewer parameters in the models improved the tolerance values and, hence, rectified the problem of multicollinearity to a certain extent. Thirdly, the estimated coefficients for the exchange rate-adjusted relative price variable (Model 2) and the exchange rate variable (Model 1) were identical in some instances for both destinations. This suggests that the effects of both factors upon tourism demand for Indonesia and Malaysia are indeed difficult, if not impossible, to separate. Due to the limitation of space, only findings for Model 2 are presented and discussed.

Tables 1 and 2 give the OLS regression results of the tourism demand equations corresponding to Model 2 for Indonesia and Malaysia, respectively. Only the final reduced models are reported. Three of the six markets for Indonesia (Japan, UK, and Germany) and one for Malaysia (USA), were re-estimated with the CORC method as a result of the presence of first-order serial correlation at the 95% confidence interval. All cases for Indonesia and Malaysia had adjusted R squared values that were statistically significant. Three models for Indonesia (Singapore, Australia, and USA) and four models for Malaysia (Japan, Singapore, Australia, and Germany) accounted for more than 90% and 80% of the variation in the dependent variable, respectively.

Income (λ_1). For Indonesia, the estimated coefficients for the income variable were statistically significant for Japan, Singapore, and Australia, and all had the expected positive signs and magnitudes that were above unity. For Malaysia, the estimated coefficient for income was statistically significant and had the expected positive sign for Japan only; the income elasticity for Japan was 2.31. The estimated income coefficient for UK was statistically significant but had a negative sign.

Relative Price (λ_2). For Indonesia, the coefficients for the exchange rate-adjusted relative price variable were significant for four of six cases (Singapore, Australia, USA, and Germany), with two cases showing the expected negative signs (Singapore and Germany). The sign of

TABLE 1. Tourism Demand Regressions (Model 2): Destination Indonesia

Origin country	Constant	ln (Income/P)	ln Exrp	Trend	DM_1	DM_2	DM_3	Adjusted R^2	DW	Estimation method
Japan	-92.59*** (-6.75)	5.74*** (6.23)	0.07 (-0.36)		0.18* (1.99)			0.74***	1.97	CORC
Singapore	29.44*** (12.85)	1.21** (2.69)	-2.25*** (5.99)					0.97***	1.46	OLS
Australia	61.71*** (15.03)	6.09*** (11.67)	0.49** (2.57)		0.33** (2.74)	0.30** (2.51)		0.95***	1.69	OLS
USA	3.73*** (-3.53)		0.72*** (4.68)	0.11*** (13.42)		N/A	-0.13* (-1.21)	0.96***	1.71	OLS
UK	7.56*** (23.10)			0.10*** (3.90)		N/A		0.47***	1.62	CORC
Germany	-9.70*** (-11.29)		-0.26* (1.87)		0.17** (2.34)			0.88***	1.58	CORC

Note. The figures in parentheses indicate t-statistics associated with the estimated coefficients.
N/A indicates that the dummy variable is not applicable in those countries.
*, **, *** indicate significance at the 90%, 95%, and 99% confidence intervals, respectively.

TABLE 2. Tourism Demand Regressions (Model 2): Destination Malaysia

Origin country	Constant	ln (Income/P)	ln Exrp	Trend	DM_1	DM_2	DM_3	DM_4	Adjusted R^2	DW	Estimation method
Japan	-41.09*** (-8.04)	2.31*** (6.76)			0.46* (2.14)			0.43** (2.65)	0.82***	1.45	OLS
Singapore	-0.45*** (-7.14)		-1.41*** (6.88)		-0.14 (-1.31)		-0.36*** (-3.20)	0.17* (2.10)	0.83***	1.86	OLS
Australia	-5.61*** (-43.40)		-1.14*** (-4.51)		-0.20 (-1.43)				0.82***	2.48	OLS
USA	-8.72 (-39.80)			0.05** (2.53)	0.20 (1.02)	N/A		0.34** (2.34)	0.54**	1.74	CORC
UK	17.83 (1.53)	-2.89* (-2.18)	-1.10*** (-4.28)	0.08** (3.18)		N/A		0.21 (1.67)	0.79***	2.16	OLS
Germany	-7.80*** (10.17)		-0.52** (-2.21)	0.02* (1.84)	0.19 (0.25)			0.38*** (3.34)	0.80***	1.85	OLS

Note. The figures in parentheses indicate t-statistics associated with the estimated coefficients.
N/A indicates that the dummy variable is not applicable in those countries.
*, **, *** indicate significance at the 90%, 95%, and 99% confidence intervals, respectively.

the relative price coefficient for Japan also was negative, although the coefficient was not significant. For Malaysia, the coefficients for the exchange rate-adjusted relative price variable were significant for four of six cases (Singapore, Australia, UK, and Germany), and all had the expected negative signs. The relative price elasticities ranged from a low of -0.52 for Germany to a high of -1.41 for Singapore.

Trend (λ_3). The trend variable was found to be significant for explaining the tourist flow patterns from USA and UK to Indonesia; both had positive coefficients and magnitudes of about 0.10. For Malaysia, the trend variable was statistically significant for USA, UK, and Germany. The coefficients were positive, and the magnitudes ranged from a low of 0.02 for Germany to a high of 0.08 for UK.

Special Events $(\lambda_4$ to $\lambda_7)$. For Indonesia, the dummy variable representing the Persian Gulf War was significant for Germany with the expected negative sign and for Australia with a positive sign. In addition, the variable also was found to be significant for Japan and had the expected negative sign. The dummy variable that accounted for the effect of the ASEAN year campaign was significant and had a positive sign for Australia only. The dummy variable representing the 1997 environmental and Asian currency crises was significant and had a negative sign for USA. For Malaysia, the dummy variable representing the 1991 Gulf War was statistically significant for Japan and had a positive sign. The dummy variable that represented the ASEAN year campaign was insignificant for all tourist-generating countries. The variable representing the 1997 crises was found to be significant for Singapore only, with the negative sign and magnitude of -0.36. The dummy variable representing the Visit Malaysia Year campaigns in 1990 and 1994 was statistically significant for Japan, Singapore, USA, and Germany, with all showing the expected positive signs. Japan had the largest coefficient value of 0.43, followed by USA at 0.34, Germany at 0.38 and Singapore at 0.17.

DISCUSSION AND IMPLICATIONS

In general, the findings affirm that income, prices, and time trend provided reasonably good explanations for the demand for Indonesian and Malaysian tourism. The relatively poor fit for the models for UK-Indonesia and USA-Malaysia suggests that other explanatory variables such as travel cost and certain non-economic factors (e.g., service quality, attractions offered, and crime rates) could be equally or more important in influencing the number of tourists from these countries. The better performance of the exchange rate-adjusted relative prices in this study (Model 2) may be an indication that most tourists from the origin countries are well aware of the joint impact of the relative CPI and exchange rates. Hence, they are driven to consider the variables collectively when making travel decisions.

The results also reveal that tourists from the same origin country responded to changes in income and prices differently, depending upon the destination country in question. Income appeared to be an important factor that affects the travel decisions of tourists from Japan, Singapore, and Australia to Indonesia. For Malaysia, the variable was important for explaining the tourist flow patterns from Japan and UK. These estimated income coefficients were consistent with previous findings (greater than one), thus confirming the view that foreign travel is a luxury product. Nevertheless, this study was not able to capture the significance of the income variable in all origin-destination country pairs primarily because of the problem of multicollinearity between the time trend and income variables in some of the models. For instance, in the case of USA-Malaysia, the correlation coefficient of the income and trend variables in the model was 0.96, indicating an approximate linear relationship between the two variables. Similarly, the negative income elasticity for the British to Malaysia was likely an indication of multicollinearity between the income and trend variables in the model (a correlation coefficient of 0.96).

The Japanese and the Australians were highly income sensitive when considering Indonesia as their vacation destination. These results imply that a heavy dependence of Indonesia for tourists from Japan and Australia will make tourism in the destination country highly vulnerable to the fluctuations of the economic conditions in Japan and Australia. Knowing that the Japanese and Australians are highly income elastic has important marketing implications for the Indonesian tourism industry. For instance, instead of mass marketing, it will be more effective for the government to target specific segments that are more economically established and stable (i.e., high-yield tourists) from Japan and Australia during the period of economic downturn. The relatively high sensitivity of the Japanese and Australians with changes in their incomes also implies that Indonesia is being perceived mostly as a competitive "sun-lust" vacation destination. This is not surprising, because a majority of tourists who visit Indonesia still head directly to Bali (Anonymous, 1993b; Anonymous, 1997a; Klapwald, 1997). Hence, one of the challenges facing the Indonesian government is to promote the country as a diverse destination, so that its tourism potential can be tapped fully.

The exchange rate adjusted-relative price is another important variable that exerts reasonably strong influence on the numbers of visitors from Singapore, Australia, USA, and Germany to Indonesia and from Singapore, Australia, UK, and Germany to Malaysia. The positive price elasticities for the Australians and Americans to Indonesia could indicate that multicollinearity was still present in the models (a correlation coefficient of -0.82 between the income and relative price variables for Australia and a correlation coefficient of -0.84 between the trend and relative price variables for USA). Singaporeans, who are better informed about the changes in prices of both destinations as a result of their close proximity, are especially sensitive toward changes in the relative prices. Similarly, Australians and British traveling to Malaysia also appear to be price elastic. These results suggest the importance of the Indonesian and Malaysian governments maintaining their prices at a level that is competitive to those in the tourist-generating countries. Therefore, policy planning with respect to the price structures of Indonesian and Malaysian goods and services related to tourism will have a substantial effect on the levels of tourist arrivals from these markets. For the Germans who are price inelastic with respect to visiting Indonesia and Malaysia, other nonprice factors (i.e., type of attractions and service quality) may be equally important for increasing their tourism demand.

Changing tastes and preferences constitute an important factor for tourist flow patterns from the USA and UK to Indonesia, as well as from the USA, UK, and Germany to Malaysia. The results suggest that Indonesia and Malaysia have become increasingly popular with these origin countries over the years. Nonetheless, behind these positive trends, there is still much room for improvement. Compared to Thailand, Indonesia is still considerably behind in successfully marketing the country as a prime vacation destination for the European and North American markets (Klapwald, 1997). One of the reasons is the limited budget available for marketing and promotion (Anonymous, 1997a). Hence, solving the funding problem should be of primary concern to the Indonesian government, and one of the best methods is to entice the private sector into entrepreneurial alliances.

The increasing popularity of Malaysia within the German market has caused the number of German tourists to increase steadily over the years. Germany appears to offer a huge growth potential for Malaysia, because the Germans alone have accounted for more than 27% of all trips taken abroad by Europeans, and they are recognized the world's biggest spenders on travel ("German market," 1998). Thus far, a number of special interest groups within the German market have been identified by the Pacific Asia Tourism Association as the most promising segments for the Asia region ("German market", 1998). Hence, future success of attracting more Germans to Malaysia rests on the government's ability to develop tourism-related products and services that specifically target these market segments.

Several special events portrayed by the dummy variables in the present study also exerted considerable impact on international tourism demand for Indonesia and Malaysia. The Persian Gulf War in 1991 resulted a 17 percent and 15 percent reductions of Japanese and German tourists to Indonesia, respectively. The Visit ASEAN campaign in 1992, on the other hand, led to a 35 percent increase in Australian tourists to Indonesia. For Malaysia, the impact of its national promotional campaigns conducted in 1990 and 1994 were particularly effective in drawing visitors from Japan, Singapore, USA, and Germany; increases ranged from 19% to 54%. However, the net effect of the 1997 forest fires and the Asian currency crisis was a 30% reduction in Singaporeans visiting Malaysia. Singapore dollars were not impacted as seriously by the currency crisis as its neighbors such as Thailand, Malaysia, and Indonesia during the year, but the economy of Singapore was somewhat adversely affected by the turmoil.

In conclusion, income, relative prices, and changing consumer preferences appear to explain the tourist flow patterns to Indonesia and Malaysia reasonably well. The estimates of the dummy variable that represents the national marketing campaigns for Malaysia imply the significance of promotional activities in influencing the number of tourist arrivals to the country.

Although it can be argued that the Indonesian and Malaysian governments have relatively limited control over some of these demand factors, the present study nonetheless identifies ways for the governments to further exploit their tourism sectors through appropriate adjustment.

This study has a few limitations. First, due to the data availability, only 18 annual data were used to develop the demand models. Hence, the reliability of these regression results may have been undermined by the lower degrees of freedom available for analysis. Similar studies with a larger number of annual observations are essential in the future to confirm the reliability of the present estimates. Second, this study was limited to the traditional tourism demand modeling approach, which implicitly assumes that tourism demand data are static (Song and Witt,

2000). However, recent attempts that examined the stationarity of the demand data have shown that many macroeconomic variables are not stationary in their levels (Lathiras and Siriopoulos, 1998; Morley, 1998; Song and Witt, 2000; Vogt and Wittayakorn, 1998; Webber, 2001), and these can lead to spurious regression problem. Hence, further research is desirable to investigate the stationarity of the variables included in the present study. In addition, in a number of origin-destination country pairs (e.g., USA and UK for Indonesia), multicollinearity problems make the resulting coefficients questionable. Therefore, readers should interpret these findings with caution. Future studies that re-specify the models in terms of first differences may help to reduce the problems (Ramanathan, 1998). Finally, the findings of the present study may be improved by considering travel costs and/or marketing variable (i.e., using total promotional expenditures spent by national tourist offices of Indonesia and Malaysia) in the models.

REFERENCES

Akis, S. (1998). A compact econometric model of tourism demand for Turkey. *Tourism Management*, 19(1), 99-102.

Anastasopoulos, P. (1989). The U.S. travel account: The impact of fluctuations of the U.S. dollar. *Hospitality Education and Research Journal*, 13(3), 469-481.

Anonymous (1993a). ASEAN travel fair: An exciting place to be. *Business Korea*, 10(11), 63.

Anonymous (1993b). Indonesia trade & investment: Tourism-Fun way to profit. *Far Eastern Economic Review*, 156(16), 58.

Anonymous (1997a, July, August). Opening new destinations. *Asiamoney (Indonesia: Emerging Opportunities Supplement)*, 63-68.

Anonymous (1997b). Promoting Malaysia. *Business Korea*, 14(8), 71.

Aznam, S. (1992). Indonesia 1992-Tourism: Growth from the Asia markets. *Far Eastern Economic Review*, 155(13), 54-56.

Bureau of Transportation Statistics: U.S. Department of Transportation (1994a). Malaysia Annual Tourism Statistical Report [Online]. Retrieved September 5, 1999 from the World Wide Web: *http://www.bts.gov/itt/T&T/getframe/malayfra.htm*

Bureau of Transportation Statistics: U.S. Department of Transportation (1994b). Visitor Arrivals to Indonesia [Online]. Retrieved September 5, 1999 from the World Wide Web: *http://www.bts.gov/itt/getframe/indo3fra.htm*

Chadee, D. & Mieczkowski, Z. (1987). An empirical analysis of the effects of the exchange rate on Canadian tourism. *Journal of Travel Research*, 26(1), 13-17.

Covington, B., Thunberg, E. M. & Jauregui, C. (1994). International demand for the U.S. as a travel destination. *Journal of Travel & Tourism Marketing*, 3(4), 39-50.

Crouch, G. I. (1994a). Guidelines for the study of international tourism demand using regression analysis. In J. R. B. Ritchie & C. R. Goeldner (Eds.), *Travel, tourism and hospitality research: A handbook for managers and researchers* (pp. 583-596). New York: John Wiley & Sons, Inc.

Crouch, G. I. (1994b). The study of international tourism demand: A review of findings. *Journal of Travel Research*, 33(1), 12-13.

Crouch, G. I. (1996). Demand elasticities in international marketing: A meta-analytical application to tourism. *Journal of Business Research*, 36, 117-136.

Crouch, G. I. (2000). An analysis of Hong Kong tourism promotion. *Asia Pacific of Tourism Research*, 5(2), 70-75.

Crouch, G. I., Schultz, L. & Valerio, P. (1992). Marketing international tourism to Australia. *Tourism Management*, 13(2), 196-208.

Di Matteo, L. & Di Matteo, R. (1993). The determinants of expenditures by Canadian visitors to the United States. *Journal of Travel Research*, 31(4), 34-42.

Dritsakis, N. & Athanasiadis, S. (2000). An econometric model of tourist demand: The case of Greece. *Journal of Hospitality & Leisure Marketing*, 7(2), 39-49.

Gerakis, A. S. (1965). Effects of exchange-rate devaluations and revaluations on receipts from tourism. *International Monetary Fund Staff Papers*, 12(3), 365-384.

German market has huge potential for Pacific Asia (1998). Hotel Online Special Report [Online]. Retrieved July 31, 1998 from the World Wide Web: http://www. hotel-online.com/Neo/News/Pres. . .ses1998_3rd/July98_PataOutboundStudy.htm

Goldsmith, A. & Zahari, M. S. (1994). Hospitality education in Malaysia: Filling the skill gap. *International Journal of Contemporary Hospitality Management*, 6(6), 27-31.

Gray, H. P. (1966). The demand for international travel by the United States and Canada. *International Economic Review*, 7(1), 83-92.

Hui, T. K. & Yuen, C. C. (1996). The effects of exchange rate, income, and habit on Japanese Travel to Canada. *Journal of Travel & Tourism Marketing*, 5(3), 265-275.

International Monetary Fund. (1998). *International Financial Statistics Yearbook*. New York: Author.

Jensen, T. (1998). Income and price elasticities by nationality for tourists in Denmark. *Tourism Economics*, 4(2), 101-130.

Jud, G. D. & Joseph, H. (1974). International demand for Latin American tourism. *Growth and Change*, 5(1), 25-31.

King, P. (1994, July/August). Growth sectors. *Corporate Location*, ss6-ss8.

Klapwald, T. (1997). The other side of the world. *World Trade*, 10(3), 49.

Kliman, M. L. (1981). A quantitative analysis of Canadian overseas tourism. *Transportation Research*, 15A(6), 487-497.

Kulendran, N. (1996). Modeling quarterly tourist flows to Australia using cointegration analysis. *Tourism Economics*, 2(3), 203-222.

Kwack, S. Y. (1972). Effects of income and prices on travel spending abroad, 1960 III-1967 IV. *International Economic Review*, 13(2), 245-255.

Lathiras, P. & Siriopoulos, C. (1998). The demand for tourism to Greece: A cointegration approach. *Tourism Economics*, 4(2), 171-185.

Lee, C. K. (1996). Major determinants of international tourism demand for South Korea: Inclusion of marketing variable. In D. R. Fesenmaier, J. T. O'Leary & M. Uysal (Eds.), *Recent advances in tourism marketing research* (pp. 101-118). New York: The Haworth Press, Inc.

Leiper, N. & Hing, N. (1998). Trends in Asia-Pacific tourism in 1997-98: from optimism to uncertainty. *International Journal of Contemporary Hospitality Management, 10*(7), 245-251.

Liden, J. & Tyler, C. (1992, August). Tourism: Stay awhile, spend some more. *Euromoney (Malaysia Supplement),*108-111,116.

Lim, C. (1997). Review of international tourism demand models. *Annals of Tourism Research, 24*(4), 835-849.

Lin, T. B. & Sung, Y. W. (1983). Hong Kong. In W. A. Pye & T. B. Lin (Eds.), *Tourism in Asia: The economic impact* (pp.50-62). Singapore: Singapore University Press.

Little, J.S. (1980, May/June). International travel in the U.S. balance of payments. *New England Economic Review*, 42-55.

Loeb, D. P. (1982). International travel to the United States: An econometric evaluation. *Annals of Tourism Research, 9*(1), 7-20.

Martin, C. A. & Witt, S. F. (1987). Tourism demand forecasting models: Choice of appropriate variable to represent tourists' cost of living. *Tourism Management, 8*(3), 233-245.

Martin, C. A. & Witt, S. F. (1988). Substitute prices in models of tourism demand. *Annals of Tourism Research, 15*(2), 255-268.

Mcbeth, J. (1994). Tourism: More than a waypoint. *Far Eastern Economic Review, 157*(17), 63.

Mohamed, N. (1995). *Conservation in Malaysia: Landscape, tourism and culture.* Unpublished doctoral dissertation, University of York, U.K.

Morley, C. L. (1994). The use of CPI for tourism prices in demand modeling. *Tourism Management, 15*(5), 342-346.

Morley, C. (1998). A dynamic international demand model. *Annals of Tourism Research, 25*(1), 70-84.

O'Hagan, J. W. & Harrison, M. J. (1984). Market shares of US tourist expenditure in Europe: An econometric analysis. *Applied Economics, 16*(6), 919-931.

Qu, H. & Lam, S. (1997). A travel demand model for Mainland Chinese tourists to Hong Kong. *Tourism Management, 18*(8), 593-597.

Ramanathan, R. (1998). *Introductory Econometrics with applications.* San Diego: The Dryden Press.

Rosensweig, J. A. (1986, July/August). Exchange rates and competition for tourism. *New England Economic Review,* 57-67.

Schansman, R. (1991). Indonesia 1991: Tourism to the archipelago. *The Cornell Hotel & Restaurant Administration Quarterly, 32*(3), 84-91.

Schwarz, A. (1988). Special report: Rebirth of an industry. *Asian Business, 24*(12), 67-69.

Selwitz, R. (1991). Southeast Asia feels war's fallout. *Hotel & Motel Management, 206*(6), 3, 52.

Soledad, G. (1996, October). Gearing for an influx. *Asiamoney (Malaysia Supplement),* 87-90.

Song, H. Y. & Witt, S. F. (2000). *Tourism demand modeling and forecasting: Modern econometric approaches.* Singapore: Pergamon.

Stronge, W. B. & Redman, M. (1982). U.S. tourism in Mexico: An empirical analysis. *Annals of Tourism Research, 9*(1), 21-35.

Summary, R. (1987). Estimation of tourism demand by multivariable regression analysis: Evidence from Kenya. *Tourism Management*, 8(4), 317-322.

United Nations Statistical Yearbook (various issues). *Department of Economics and Social Affairs Statistics Division*. New York: Author.

Uysal, M. & Crompton, J. L. (1984). Determinants of demand for international tourist flows to Turkey. *Tourism Management*, 5(4), 288-297.

Vogt, M. & Wittayakorn, C. (1998). Determinants of the demand for Thailand's export of tourism. *Applied Economics*, 30, 711-715.

Webber, A. (2001). Exchange rate volatility and cointegration in tourism demand. *Journal of Travel Research*, 39(2), 398-405.

Witt, S. F. & Martin, C. A. (1987). Deriving a relative price index for inclusion in international tourism demand estimation models: Comment. *Journal of Travel Research*, 25(3), 38-40.

Witt, S. F. & Martin, C. A. (1987). Econometric models for forecasting international tourism demand. *Journal of Travel Research*, 25(3), 23-30.

Witt, S. F. & Witt, C. A. (1992). Tourism demand: Literature review and econometric model specification. In *Modeling and forecasting demand in tourism* (pp. 16-29). San Diego: Academic Press Inc.

Witt, S. F. & Witt, C. A. (1995). Forecasting tourism demand: A review of empirical research. *International Journal of Forecasting*, 11(3), 447-475.

World Tourism Organization (1998). WTO Statistical Database [Online]. Retrieved June 15, 1998 from the World Wide Web: http://www.world-tourism.org/esta/statserv.htm

Determinants of Domestic
Travel Expenditure in South Korea

Woo Gon Kim
Hailin Qu

SUMMARY. This study examines factors affecting domestic Korean tourist expenditure per person. Independent variables include family size, Per Capita Gross National Product (GNP), number of cars, number of working hours, number of years of education, previous year's domestic travel expenditure, and exchange rate. A 21-year historical data were used in the study. Two estimation methods, principal components regression and ridge regression, were employed in this study to eliminate the problems of multicollinearity caused by Ordinary Least Squares (OLS) method. The empirical results show that number of working hours, family size, and number of years of education turned out to be important factors affecting domestic travel expenditure. *[Article copies available for a fee from The Haworth Document Delivery Service: 1-800-HAWORTH. E-mail address: <getinfo@haworthpressinc.com> Website: <http://www.HaworthPress.com> © 2002 by The Haworth Press, Inc. All rights reserved.]*

Woo Gon Kim is Assistant Professor in the School of Hotel and Restaurant Administration, Oklahoma State University, Stillwater, OK, USA. Hailin Qu is Professor in the School of Hotel and Restaurant Administration, Oklahoma State University, Stillwater, OK, USA.

Address correspondence to: Woo Gon Kim, School of Hotel and Restaurant Administration, Oklahoma State University, 210 HESW, Stillwater, OK 74078-6173 USA (E-mail: kwoo@okstate.edu).

[Haworth co-indexing entry note]: "Determinants of Domestic Travel Expenditure in South Korea." Kim, Woo Gon, and Hailin Qu. Co-published simultaneously in *Journal of Travel & Tourism Marketing* (The Haworth Hospitality Press, an imprint of The Haworth Press, Inc.) Vol. 13, No. 1/2, 2002, pp. 85-97; and: *Tourism Forecasting and Marketing* (ed: Kevin K. F. Wong and Haiyan Song) The Haworth Hospitality Press, an imprint of The Haworth Press, Inc., 2002, pp. 85-97. Single or multiple copies of this article are available for a fee from The Haworth Document Delivery Service [1-800-HAWORTH, 9:00 a.m. - 5:00 p.m. (EST). E-mail address: getinfo@haworthpressinc.com].

KEYWORDS. Travel expenditure, tourism demand, domestic travel, South Korea, multicollinearity, principal components regression, ridge regression

INTRODUCTION

Finding out factors affecting tourism demand is important task for planning, policymaking, and budgeting purposes by tourism operators, investors, and government organizations concerned with tourism. With the rapid national economic growth, domestic travel demand has increased dramatically in South Korea. In 1997, approximately 31 million people participated in daily leisure travel and overnight leisure travel. That figure was slightly over 87 percent of total population over 13 years old. Average leisure travel frequency per person was 6.61 times per year in 1996, while that figure was 5.3 times in 1994. Average travel days per person recorded 9.1 days in 1996, while that figure was 7.37 days in 1994 (KNTC, 1997). Domestic travel expenditure per person in 1996 recorded approximately US\$252 (equivalent to 252,000 Korean won), while that figure was US\$233 (233,000 won) in 1994. From 1980 to 1996, the number of domestic travels increased at almost 11.8% annual compound rate. The rapid increase of demand is likely to be related to the factors such as Per Capita Gross National Product (GNP), leisure time, number of automobiles, family size, number of years of education, and exchange rate.

The tourism demand among West European and North American countries has dominated the research (Crouch, 1994). With a few exceptions (Japan and Australia), however, the tourism demand in most of Asia and the Pacific destinations have largely been ignored or have not fully explored. It is the same situation in Korea. The limited number of Korea domestic tourism researches have been conducted and it has not been given much attention until recently.

The purpose of this study is to find out factors affecting the demand that is expressed in Per Capita expenditure.

LITERATURE REVIEW

Numerous studies were done to estimate international tourism demand measured as travel expenditure or number of tourists. Quayson and Var (1982) used log-linear regression models to estimate tourism demand of an area of British Columbia. National income, a relative price index, distance, and cross exchange rates were used as explanatory variables, while international tourist expenditure was used as a response variable. Shulmeister (1979) lists the following variables as being the most important exogenous variables in an econometric model of tourism demand: disposable income of private households, Per Capita GNP, private consumption, prices of consumer goods, tourism prices, transportation costs, consumer economic expectation, relative prices between domestic and foreign countries. O'Hagen and Harrison (1984) included marketing expenditure in the demand model and analyzed econometrically the evolution of market shares of U.S. tourist expenditure in Europe.

Crouch (1994) found that Ordinary Least Squares (OLS) multiple regression has been used most to study the determinants of demand for international tourism. Previous tourism demand studies identified many of the exogenous variables that could be used to explain tourism demand and the most commonly used exogenous variables were: (1) the levels of income of the potential tourists; (2) relative price levels in the two countries and in alternative destinations; (3) the cost of travel from the point of origin to the destination; and (4) the currency exchange rate (Crouch, 1994). The results varied considerably across the tourism demand studies under different conditions such as different country or region and different methodology employed. However, in general, it was found that "Income" was a highly relevant explanatory variable and most international travel was highly income elastic; "Relative Prices" were significant determinants and had a strong influence on travel demand; "Exchange Rate" was consistently a significant factor but had a modest impact on tourism demand; and "Transportation Cost" was generally not a significant or major determinant in tourism demand. Moreover, some dummy variables were shown to have impacts on tourism demand. Such variables might include political factors, special events, travel restrictions, and other disturbances that were difficult to quantify (Crouch, 1994).

Syriopoulos and Sinclair (1993) estimated the Almost Ideal Demand System (AIDS) model for four European origin countries and they applied the AIDS model to a specific group of Mediterranean countries. Lim (1999) provided a meta analysis of more than 70 previous empirical studies. He showed the relationships between international tourism demand and the important explanatory variables (income, transportation costs, and tourism prices). Song et al. (2000) did an empirical study of outbound tourism demand in the U.K. and estimated outbound tourist demand models according to the 12 holiday destinations of U.K. residents.

Kim (1996) investigated the factors affecting leisure-related expenditure of the Korean household. Included as independent variables in his study are family size, working hours per week, urbanization rate, number of years of education, and Per Capita GNP. The empirical results of his study show that Per Capita GNP turned out to be the most significant variable affecting leisure-related expenditure. To the best of our knowledge, this study is the first attempt to find out factors affecting domestic travel expenditure in Korea. The purpose of the study was to develop a demand model and to identify the exogenous variables that best explained the travel demand of domestic Korean tourist expenditure. Very few studies were done on this topic regarding factors affecting domestic travel expenditure. In Korea, no previous study was conducted to identify the determining factors of domestic travel expenditure. That would be mainly attributed to the lack of domestic travel expenditure data.

DATA SOURCE AND MODEL SPECIFICATION

Data Source

A 21-year historical data were used in this study. Domestic travel expenditure data were collected from the survey results of Korea National Tourism Corporation (KNTC) during the period of 1976 to 1996. Since the expenditure data for the entire period were not available, missing data for several years were estimated through interpolation technique. Other data related to explanatory variables were collected from the Bureau of Statistics and other government organizations.

Variable Specification

The dependent variable was domestic travel expenditure per person. The explanatory variables used in the study were the previous year's expenditure, Per Capita GNP, family size, number of cars, number of working hours, number of years of education and exchange rate. Previous year's expenditure was used as a lagged variable since this year's domestic travel expenditure was usually affected by previous year's expenditure. Exchange rate was included in this study, because exchange rate is likely to affect Korean overseas tourist expenditure that is likely to have a substitutive relationship with domestic travel expenditure. Number of cars was included in this study, because it was perceived as an important variable that have had a direct impact on the number of domestic trips and domestic travel expenditure. Due to the relatively small size of the country, increasing number of automobiles have provided high mobility and tourists have had better and fast access to many destinations, as compared to the traditional transportation, namely, train and tour bus.

Model Specification

First, the ordinary least squares (OLS) regression model was used to determine which factors affected travel expenditure. The OLS regression technique estimates the parameter betas by minimizing the sum of squares of the error terms. The following model is suggested.

$$\ln TR = \beta_0 + \beta_1 \ln TR1 + \beta_2 \ln GNP + \beta_3 \ln FS + \beta_4 \ln CAR + \beta_5 \ln WT + \beta_6 \ln EL + \varepsilon$$

where:

$\ln TR$	natural log of domestic travel expenditure per person in U.S. dollar;
$\ln TR1$	natural log of previous year's domestic travel expenditure per person in U.S. dollar;
$\ln GNP$	natural log of Per Capita GNP in U.S. dollar;
$\ln FS$	natural log of family size: number of persons per household;
$\ln CAR$	natural log of number of cars per household;
$\ln WT$	natural log of number of working hours per week;
$\ln EL$	natural log of number of years of education;
$\ln ER$	natural log of exchange rate U.S.\$ versus Korean won; and
ε	error terms

The expected signs of regression coefficients are as follows. Variables including previous year's expenditure, Per Capita GNP, number of cars per household, number of years of education, exchange rate are expected to have a positive sign, while the remaining two variables, number of persons per household and number of working hours per week, are expected to show a negative sign. Due to the rapid industrialization, family size decreased and each family member now has more leisure time and higher disposable income than before. The number of persons per household decreased more than one person in past 20 years. In 1996, the number of persons per household was 3.57 comparing 4.83 in 1977. Therefore, it is expected that decreasing family size would have a positive impact on domestic travel expenditure. In other words, each household will spend more on per person basis. By the same token, number of working hours per week is expected to show a negative relationship with domestic travel expenditure. Average working hours per week were 47.3 hours in 1997 and decreased from 52.4 hours per week in 1976. Reduced number of working hours per week is likely to allow more travel that will lead to increasing travel expenditure.

EMPIRICAL RESULTS

The above section described a number of variables and their indicators affecting domestic travel expenditure. The OLS regression was used to estimate the domestic travel expenditure. The regression results are presented in Table 1.

The OLS expenditure model (Model 1) turned out to be significant at 1% level or better with R^2 of 0.98 or better. Model 1 includes all 7 ex-

TABLE 1. OLS Regression Results (Model 1)

Variable	Expected Sign	Coefficient (t-value)	T-Value
TR1	+	1.0459	5.81**
GNP	+	−1.1745	−0.31
FS	−	9.5244	3.00**
CAR	+	.1967	0.30
WT	−	.7489	0.20
EL	+	5.9054	1.11
ER	+	−.0976	−0.18
Intercept		−26.901	−1.66
R2		.9899	
Standard error		0.1107	

*p ≤ .05. **p ≤ .01.*

planatory variables described above. In Model 1, the signs of four explanatory variables, Per Capita GNP, family size, working hours and exchange rate, were not as expected. Although the coefficient of determination (R^2) was very high (.9899), only two explanatory variables turned out to be significant at 5% level in Model 1. It is the typical symptom of the multicollinearity that shows a high R^2 but a few significant t ratios (Gujarati, 1995).

Detection of Multicollinearity

Another suggested way to detect multicollinearity is to use the pair-wise correlation coefficients between two regressors. If the correlation coefficients are high, then multicollinearity may be existed. The correlation matrix among variables is displayed in Table 2.

Domestic travel expenditure turned out to have a very large positive correlation with previous year's domestic travel expenditure (TR1), Per Capita GNP (GNP), number of cars per household (CAR), and number of years of education (EL). Per Capita GNP showed a very high negative correlation with family size (FS), and positive correlation with number of cars per household, and number of years of education (EL). In general, as family size decreases, disposable income per person increases, people are able to own more cars and have higher education. Table 2 shows that family size has a high negative correlation with number of cars per household and number of years of education. As family size decreases, the number of cars owned by household and number of years of education increases. Since the pair-wise correlation coefficient between two independent variables is very high, it is

TABLE 2. Correlation Matrix Between Variables in Model 1

Variable	TR	TR1	GNP	FS	CAR	WT	EL	ER
TR	1.00	.98447	.92644	−.92162	.95031	−.84344	.91835	.56046
TR1		1.00	.91912	−.93274	.93378	−.79255	.90865	.59187
GNP			1.00	−.98913	.98520	−.78714	.99780	.68143
FS				1.00	−.97301	.75347	−.98864	−.68606
CAR					1.00	−.87423	.98396	.56630
WT						1.00	−.78466	−.17182
YE							1.00	.68335
ER								1.00

suspected that serious multicollinearity may exist in the OLS regression.

The indicators of multicollinearity that have been described above can be obtained using standard regression computations. The other way to detect multicollinearity requires some calculations that are not usually included in standard regression packages. The analysis follows from the fact that every linear regression model can be restated in terms of a set of orthogonal explanatory variables. They are referred to as the principal components of the explanatory set of variables (Chatterjee and Price, 1977).

Principal components were derived from original variables or standardized variables. A standardized variable is obtained by subtracting the average value from each observation and dividing it by the standard deviation of the observations. The number of principal components is same as the number of original explanatory variables. The variance of principal components is called eigenvalue (λ). Each principal component is arranged in the descending order of eigenvalue. Table 3 represent eigenvalues and condition indexes of Model.

If any one of the λ's is exactly equal to zero, there is perfect linear relationship among the original variables which exhibits an extreme case of multicollinearity. If one of the λ's is much smaller than the others and near zero, multicollinearity is present. It is known that weak dependencies are associated with condition indexes around 5 or 10, whereas moderate to strong relations are associated with condition indexes of 30 to 100 (Belsey et al., 1980). Condition index represents the collinearity of combinations of variables in the data set. To diagnose the variables with high multicollinearity, all condition indexes above a threshold value are identified with 30 the most commonly used value. Then for all condition indexes exceeding the threshold, a collinearity problem is indicated when more than two variables have variance proportions above 90 percent (Hair et al., 1992).

TABLE 3. Eigenvalues of Model 1

	PC1	PC2	PC3	PC4	PC5	PC6	PC7	SUM
Eigenvalues (λ)	5.9448	.85747	.11524	.07361	.00649	.00177	.00065	7.0000
Condition indexes (CI)	1.0000	2.6330	7.1824	8.9869	30.277	57.967	95.770	

Results of Principal Components (PC) Regression and Ridge Regression

Principal components (PC) regression is used to remedy severe multicollinearity problem in OLS regression. The specific procedures of performing PC regression are as follows. First, principal components are derived. Second, a few principal components were selected and used as independent variables. Two principle components were selected in this study. The regression coefficients of above selected variables were estimated by OLS. Third, the estimated regression coefficients derived from second step were applied to calculate the regression coefficients of standardized variables. Fourth, the regression coefficients of the standardized variables were converted into those of the original variables.

Ridge regression is another method that has been proposed to remedy multicollinearity problems by modifying the method of ordinary least squares to allow biased estimators of the regression coefficients. The ridge regression coefficients are calculated by the following formula:

$$\beta_{\scriptscriptstyle L} = [X'X + kI]^{-1}X'Y$$

When k is greater than 0, the ridge regression coefficients are biased but tend to be more stable than ordinary least squares estimators. A commonly used method of determining the constant k is based on the ridge trace. The ridge trace is a simultaneous plot of the values of the estimated ridge standardized regression coefficients for different values of k, usually between 0 and 1. An estimated regression coefficient tend to fluctuate widely as k is changed slightly from 0, but these wide fluctuations cease and the magnitude of the regression coefficient tends to change very slowly as k is increased further (Neter et al., 1990). In this study, the optimal k value was found to be 0.6, which is relatively large. Based on this value, the estimated regression coefficients became stable in the ridge trace. The results of PC regression and ridge regression are presented in Table 4.

Major problems found in OLS regression (Model 1) were solved by running PC and ridge regression (Model 2). The signs of all explanatory variables were correct and contradictory signs were eliminated. In addition, t-values of most explanatory variables turned out to be large and significant. Results of PC and ridge regression resulted in being quite

TABLE 4. Regression Results by PC Regression and Ridge Regression (Model 2)

Variable	Expected Sign	PC Regression	Ridge Regression
		Coefficient (t-value)	Coefficient (t-value)
TR1	+	.1667 (14.19)**	.2498 (7.12)**
GNP	+	.1580 (13.74)**	.1176 (7.07)**
FS	−	−1.5402 (−12.70)**	−1.1765 (−5.84)**
CAR	+	.1226 (12.13)**	.0978 (9.50)**
WT	−	4.3205 (−4.78)**	−3.4396 (−4.52)**
EL	+	1.0567 (13.60)**	.7332 (6.15)**
ER	+	.0441 (.17)	.2335 (1.21)
Intercept		.9122 (2.93)**	14.484 (3.93)**
R2		.9758	.9329
Standard error		0.1437	0.2846
Durbin-Watson Statistic		1.98	1.82

* p ≤ .05. ** p ≤ .01.

similar even though both methods are based on quite different analytical approach.

In order to detect the presence of first-order autocorrelation among the residuals of this sample, Durbin-Watson d statistic was used. The d statistic is 1.82 for -Ridge regression and 1.98 for PC regression (see Table 4). Since both d statistics are above d_u, it can be concluded that the error terms (residuals) of time series data are not autocorrelated.

According to the result of PC regression represented in Table 4, the number of working hours per week (WT, $\beta = -4.32$, $p \le 0.01$) turned out to be the most important variable affecting domestic travel expenditure followed by number of persons per household (FS, $\beta = -1.54$, $p \le 0.01$) and number of years of education (EL, $\beta = 1.06$, $p \le 0.01$). In this study, regression coefficients are directly interpreted as level of elasticity because natural log of both explanatory and dependent variables are used. As the number of working hours and number of persons per household decrease by 1%, expenditure increases by 4.32% and 1.54%, respectively. The expenditure increases by 1.06% as the number of years of education increases by 1%. Therefore, the above three explanatory variables turned out to be elastic since the elasticity is greater than unity. However, previous year's expenditure (TR1) and Per Capita GNP turned out to be inelastic. As both previous year's expenditure and

Per Capita GNP increase by 1%, expenditure increases by 0.17% and
0.16%, respectively. The elasticity level of these two variables may increase if those variables such as number of working hours, number of
persons per household, and number of years of education were not included in the model. Seemingly, the important variable such as exchange rate was not a significant variable. It is mainly because of the
fact that exchange rate in Korea used to be very stable for a long period
of time until recent years' rate increase.

It is postulated that domestic travel expenditure is negatively affected
by overseas travel and will be a substitute of overseas travel. In other
words, more Korean travelers will select domestic destinations rather
than overseas destinations if exchange rate increases and the value of
Korean won decreases. Many tourists tended to plan overseas travel in
advance, thus, the substitution effect of overseas travel is quite weak
and domestic travel demand is not much affected by increasing overseas travel.

CONCLUSION

This study investigated factors affecting Korea domestic travel expenditure per person. Explanatory variables include family size, Per
Capita GNP, number of cars, number of working hours, number of
years of education, previous year's expenditure, and exchange rate.

Due to the severe multicollinearity problems in OLS regression
model (Model 1), two alternative estimation methods, principal components (PC) regression and ridge regression, were used as remedial
measures in this study. PC and ridge regression showed a dramatic improvement of multicollinearity over OLS regression. Conflicting sign
problem disappeared and the number of significant explanatory variables increased.

The empirical results showed that number of working hours per week
(WT) turned out to be the most important variable affecting domestic
travel expenditure followed by number of persons per household (FS)
and number of years of education (EL). As the number of working
hours per person increased, people tend to have less leisure time for
traveling, which led to lower expenditures. In general, blue-color workers in South Korea tend to work much longer than white-color workers.
This study showed a strongly significant negative correlation between
number of working hours per person and Per Capita GNP. Blue-color
workers tend to work more and are likely to have fewer days of pleasure

travel, since their discretionary income is lower than white-color counterparts. Number of years of education turned out to have a high positive correlation with Per Capita GNP and number of cars. Highly educated people turned out to have higher income and more cars as compared to people with lower education. Therefore, people with higher number of years of education are more likely to spend more on travel expenditure due to higher income and mobility. Since many destinations such as ski resorts, mountain resorts, beach resorts are only accessible by automobile, travel expenditure will increase when the number of people owning their vehicles increases.

However, there is a major limitation in this study. Since several years' data were not available during the 21 years period, the missing years' data were estimated through interpolation technique. It might have caused the problem of the robustness of the domestic tourism demand analysis.

Domestic travel expenditure was hypothesized to have a negative relationship with the frequency of overseas travel. Domestic travel is considered be a substitute for overseas travel. More Korean pleasure travelers will select domestic destinations rather than overseas destinations if the value of the Korean won becomes weak relative to other currencies. Seemingly important exchange rate variable resulted in not being a significant one. That is mainly because of the fact that exchange rate in Korea was very stable for a long period of time from 1976 and 1996. However, since the Asian financial crisis in 1998, substitution effect could have been significant if the model used more recent data set. For example, it is not uncommon to find that many just married couples selected domestic destination as their honeymoon trip, as compared to the past trends that a higher percentage of newly-married couples chose their honeymoon trips abroad.

The findings of this study indicated that the travel demand and travel expenditure of South Korean tourists showed unique results that do not necessarily follow the Western model of tourism demand. In addition, this study showed that the explanatory variables such as number of working hours per week (WT), number of persons per household (FS), number of years of education (EL), Per Capita GNP (GNP), previous year's travel expenditure per person (TR1), number of cars per household (CAR) significantly affected the domestic travel expenditure in South Korea. However, exchange rate was not a significant variable affecting domestic tourism demand.

REFERENCES

Belsey, D.A., E. Kuh, & R.E. Welsch (1980), Regression Diagnostics: Identifying Influential Data and Sources of Collinearity, Wiley.

Chatterjee, S. and B. Price (1977), Regression Analysis By Example, Wiley.

Crouch, G. (1994, February). The Study of International Tourism Demand: A Survey of Practice. *Journal of Travel Research*, 32(3), 41-55.

Crouch, G. (1994, Summer). The Study of International Tourism Demand: A Review of Findings. *Journal of Travel Research*, 32(4), 12-23.

Gujarati, D.N. (1995), Basic Econometrics, McGraw-Hill.

Hair, J., Anderson, R., Tatham, R. & Black, W. (1992). Multivariate Data Analysis (2nd ed.). New York: Macmillan Publishing Company.

Kim, K.H. (1996), "An Analysis on the Determinants of Increasing Leisure-related Expenditure," Journal of Tourism Sciences, 19(2): 117-131.

Korea National Tourism Corporation, Annual Report on Domestic Tourism, 1997.

Lim, C. (1999, February). A Meta-Analytic Review of International Tourism Demand. *Journal of Travel Research*, 37(3), 273-284.

Neter, J., W. Wasserman & M. Kutner (1990), Applied Linear Statistical Models, Irwin.

O'Hagen, J.W. and M.J. Harrison (1984), "Market Shares of U.S. Tourist Expenditure in Europe: An Econometric Analysis," Applied Economics, 16: 919-931.

Papatheodorou, A. (1999). The Demand for International Tourism in the Mediterranean Region. *Applied Economics*, 31, 619-630.

Quayson, J. and T. Var (1982), "The Tourism Demand Function For the Okanagan, B.C," International Journal of Tourism Management, 3: 108-115.

Shulmeister, S. (1979), Tourism and The Business Cycle, Austrian Institute for Economic Research.

Song, H., Romilly, P., & Liu, X. (2000). An Empirical Study of Outbound Tourism Demand in the UK. *Applied Economics*, 32, 611-624.

Syriopoulos, T. & Sinclair, M. (1993). An Econometric Study of Tourism Demand: the AIDS Model of US and European Tourism in Mediterranean Countries. *Applied Economics*, 25, 1541-1552.

Trends and Forecasts
for Inbound Tourism to China

Stephen F. Witt
Lindsay W. Turner

SUMMARY. The development of tourism in China over the last two decades is reviewed. It is argued that the success of the economic reforms in China which has resulted in fast economic growth has also been the main cause of rapid tourism growth in China. Forecasts of international tourist arrivals by source country market and destination region within China are generated over the period 2001-05. An integrative approach is used which combines both time-series and econometric methodologies, termed structural integrated time-series econometric analysis (SITEA). *[Article copies available for a fee from The Haworth Document Delivery Service: 1-800-HAWORTH. E-mail address: <getinfo@haworthpressinc.com> Website: <http://www.HaworthPress.com> © 2002 by The Haworth Press, Inc. All rights reserved.]*

KEYWORDS. Economic reforms, tourism development, tourism forecasts, China

---

Stephen F. Witt is Chair of Tourism Forecasting, School of Management, University of Surrey, Guildford, UK. Lindsay W. Turner is Professor in Econometrics and Head of School of Applied Economics, Victoria University, Melbourne, Australia.

Address correspondence to: Stephen F. Witt, School of Management, University of Surrey, Guildford GU2 7XH UK (E-mail: a.west@surrey.ac.uk).

The authors are grateful to Haiyan Song for the provision of information on China.

[Haworth co-indexing entry note]: "Trends and Forecasts for Inbound Tourism to China." Witt, Stephen F., and Lindsay W. Turner. Co-published simultaneously in *Journal of Travel & Tourism Marketing* (The Haworth Hospitality Press, an imprint of The Haworth Press, Inc.) Vol. 13, No. 1/2, 2002, pp. 99-109; and: *Tourism Forecasting and Marketing* (ed: Kevin K. F. Wong and Haiyan Song) The Haworth Hospitality Press, an imprint of The Haworth Press, Inc., 2002, pp. 99-109. Single or multiple copies of this article are available for a fee from The Haworth Document Delivery Service [1-800-HAWORTH, 9:00 a.m. - 5:00 p.m. (EST). E-mail address: getinfo@haworthpressinc.com].

INTRODUCTION

China has experienced spectacular economic growth since the start of its economic reforms. During the period 1978-88, which was the first phase of the economic reforms, China's economic growth averaged 10.1% per year, while the average economic growth rates in developing and developed economies over the same period were only 3.4% and 2.7%, respectively. From 1989-97, the average growth rate of the Chinese economy was 9.1% per annum, which was again the highest among both developing and developed economies during the period. Although in 1998 and 1999 China was affected by the financial crisis in Southeast Asia, its economy still recorded 7.8% and 7.1% growth rates, respectively. The real GDP of China in 2000 was ranked seventh largest in the world as measured by the Yuan/US dollar exchange rate, and second largest (after the USA) in terms of purchasing power parity.

It is widely known that the recent success of the Chinese economy has been mainly due to the success of the economic reforms in China. China's fast economic growth took place from the base of a socialist economy where production, consumption, investment, imports and exports were all tightly controlled by the central government. This socialist economy was at the edge of total destruction just after the Cultural Revolution. Increasing pressures were being built up both from within and outside China to reform the centrally planned economy. Chai (1998) identified three main reasons why China started its economic reforms. Firstly, the planned system was causing increased inefficiency in the use of resources. An overall indicator of the inefficient use of resources was the declining total factor productivity (TFP). According to Yeh (1984), the growth of the TFP was negative during and immediately after the Cultural Revolution. With a declining TFP, economic growth in China could only be achieved through an increase in labour and/or capital inputs. The increase in capital input led to a reduction in consumption and worsening living standards. The expansion of labour inputs resulted in a decline in leisure time. Both of these reduced consumers' welfare in China, and this put considerable pressure on the communist party to start the economic reforms. Secondly, modernization is regarded as an important goal in China, and hence there was pressure for economic reforms to close the gap between China and the advanced economies. The then Chinese government realized that this could only be done through economic reforms to increase the number of China's own innovations and/or to facilitate technology transfer from advanced economies. Thirdly, the disequilibrium of the economy had increased significantly due to the planned system. It was clear not only that the government could not deliver long-term sustained economic growth, but it was also incapable of co-ordinating demand and supply effectively. This situation was further exacerbated by the imbalance between heavy industry and other sectors of the economy, as the a result of the government's adoption of heavy industry-oriented development strategies.

The reforms in China may be divided into three distinct but inter-related phases. The first phase was from 1978-84, during which only partial reforms, mainly in the rural areas, were introduced. The objective of these reforms was to introduce incentives for farming through decentralizing property rights and the abolition of the commune system. Although efforts were also made to increase the autonomy of, and financial incentives for, state owned and collectively owned enterprises, the scale of the reforms was very small. The open-door policy was also initiated during this period with the intention to encourage international trade and foreign direct investment in China.

The second phase of the reforms relates to the period 1985-91. During this period the reform focus shifted from the rural areas to urban areas. A comprehensive enterprise reform program was introduced to transform the planned economy into a market economy. The reforms included the following: reducing the scope of government planning; strengthening enterprise autonomy and accountability; liberalizing product and factor prices; and creating both product and factor markets. At the macro level, the Chinese government also made an effort to utilize monetary and fiscal policy to regulate the economy, which had not been possible under the planned system.

The third phase of the reforms was from 1992 onwards. During this period China abandoned the planned system and adopted the full market economic mechanism. The changes included further enhancing the incentive mechanism in state owned enterprises, removing production price control, and establishing two financial markets in order to channel scarce resources to the most productive sectors. The open-door policy was once again reinforced and widely implemented across all sectors of the economy including the tourism industry, as well as foreign trade, banking and insurance.

TOURISM DEVELOPMENT

The reform-induced economic growth also led to rapid development of the tourism sector in China. International tourist arrivals in 1978 were only 1.8 million, but this figure reached 63.5 million in 1998 (including foreign tourists, overseas Chinese and visitors from Hong Kong, Chinese Taipei and Macau), giving an average annual growth rate of 18.5%. International tourism receipts in 1978 were a mere US$263 million, but reached US$12.6 billion in 1998 (China National Tourism Administration, 1999). The corresponding average annual growth rate was 20.2%.

The reforms in the tourism sector were broadly in line with those in other industries, and the main objectives of the reforms were to increase enterprise autonomy and managerial efficiency. These goals were achieved through the decentralization of tourism pricing and the introduction of incentive systems for tourism enterprises. During the period 1978-93, the prices of some tourism products and services were allowed to vary according to market demand, but the prices of the majority of tourism products and services were still under the control of the central and/or provincial governments. Since 1994, however, tourism enterprises have been given the full right to decide their own prices based purely on demand in both domestic and international tourism markets (Zhang et al., 1998). The first major incentive scheme introduced in the tourism industry was the contract responsibility system, under which a tourism enterprise was allowed to retain all or most of its excess profit after a given amount of obligatory delivery of revenues to the government. The second incentive system was a bonus scheme for employees and managerial personnel. This scheme linked the performance of a tourism enterprise to the incomes of its employees and managers, and hence both employees and managers were motivated to improve the quality and variety of tourism products and services according to the rules of the market economy. All these reforms have played an important role in the recent rapid growth of the tourism industry in China.

Although market forces have been the key determinant in the recent development of China's tourism industry, the role of government should not be ignored. Zhang et al. (1999) argue that the rapid growth of international tourism in China can also be attributed to the policies adopted by the Chinese government. The government gradually gave up its role as sole central planner for the tourism industry during the reform period. In particular, the Chinese government has been acting as a regulator in formulating and implementing positive and forward looking tourism policies; as an investment stimulator to encourage investment in the tourism sector through improving financial incentives for both public and private investors; as a promoter to promote China as an international destination world-wide; as a co-ordinator to liase with different departments within the government in relation to tourism development; and as educator to provide tourism-related education and training to meet the needs of the tourism industry.

China's tourism industry faced a big challenge when several major tourism source countries such as Indonesia, Korea, Malaysia, the Philippines and Thailand were hit hard by the financial crisis from mid-1997. According to the World Tourism Organization (WTO, 1999), more than 55% of inbound tourist arrivals in China during the period 1993-97 were from southeast Asian countries. With economic problems in these countries, inbound tourist arrivals declined substantially in 1998. For example, compared with 1997, tourist arrivals from Indonesia, Korea, Malaysia, the Philippines and Thailand in 1998 dropped by 29%, 19%, 16%, 7% and 14%, respectively. However, tourist arrivals from Europe, North America and Australia increased significantly, with growth rates ranging from 5% to 13%. As a result net increases in international tourist arrivals and tourism receipts still took place in 1998, with growth rates of 10% and 4%, respectively.

FORECASTS

During 1999, tourism to China grew rapidly. The increase from 1998 to 1999 was 18.6% (excluding Hong Kong), with growth from the Americas of 8.8%, Europe 10.1% and Asia Pacific 25.7%. In the Asia Pacific region, particularly strong growth occurred for South Korea, Australia and Thailand, and can in part be attributed to China receiving tourists who switched from the troubled market of Indonesia and away from more expensive European and North American destinations.

Turner and Witt (2000) have published tourism forecasts for the Asia Pacific region using data up to 1998 to estimate the models, and in this paper the forecasts for China have been updated to incorporate the 1999 actual tourist arrivals figures from the various source countries. The new forecasts are presented in Table 1. Arrivals in China from Chinese Taipei, Hong Kong and Macau are not forecast, and are not included in the totals.

The forecasts are generated using an integrative approach combining both time-series and econometric methodologies, termed structural integrated time-series econometric analysis (SITEA). Firstly, trend and cyclical components are fitted to the data series, and, secondly, the influences of economic and dummy variables are examined. A time-series approach has the advantage of overcoming the problems associated

TABLE 1. Forecast International Tourist Arrivals in China by Source Market 2001-2005

Market	1999 Actual	2001	2002	2005
Americas				
Canada	213699	291390	351790	392710
USA	736386	883570	887200	1033300
Total Americas	950085	1174960	1238990	1426010
Europe				
France	156640	193190	214540	262100
Germany	217632	260960	285760	335680
Italy	72216	90536	101988	131370
Netherlands	70084	97616	115450	162100
Portugal	40221	43819	44755	46197
Sweden	46788	55128	60421	73100
UK	258894	280740	288590	303500
Total Europe	862475	1021989	1111504	1314047
Asia Pacific				
Australia	203539	239080	253870	288400
India	84203	111750	130680	208980
Indonesia	182904	181670	188460	202530
Japan	1865200	2148400	2324500	2779200
North Korea	69819	67898	68616	70123
Malaysia	372870	375580	381390	426800
Myanmar	33263	33992	34096	34382
New Zealand	31440	38384	39121	49778
Philippines	298285	321620	332140	351750
Singapore	352479	398930	412830	434080
South Korea	991979	1200300	1289400	1484200
Thailand	206424	252340	279000	342100
Vietnam	51894	71378	78994	93981
Other Asia Pacific	426423	523626	546600	619819
Total Asia Pacific	5170722	5964948	6359697	7386123
Other Markets	1449014	1669023	1805829	2159071
Total	8432296	9830920	10516020	12285251

Note: Chinese Taipei, Hong Kong and Macau are not included.

with spurious regression, and will tend in many cases to generate accurate forecasts, but such an approach by itself is limiting, especially in understanding the economic forces that are behind the changes in the flow series. The SITEA model as outlined in Figure 1 uses a time-series approach as a starting point. In this process the underlying series is fitted to form a mathematical projection of the cyclical and trend components, where present, and then the influence of economic variables is added sequentially to adjust these time-series components. Further, dummy variables can be added under the judgment of the forecaster to

FIGURE 1. SITEA Modeling Process

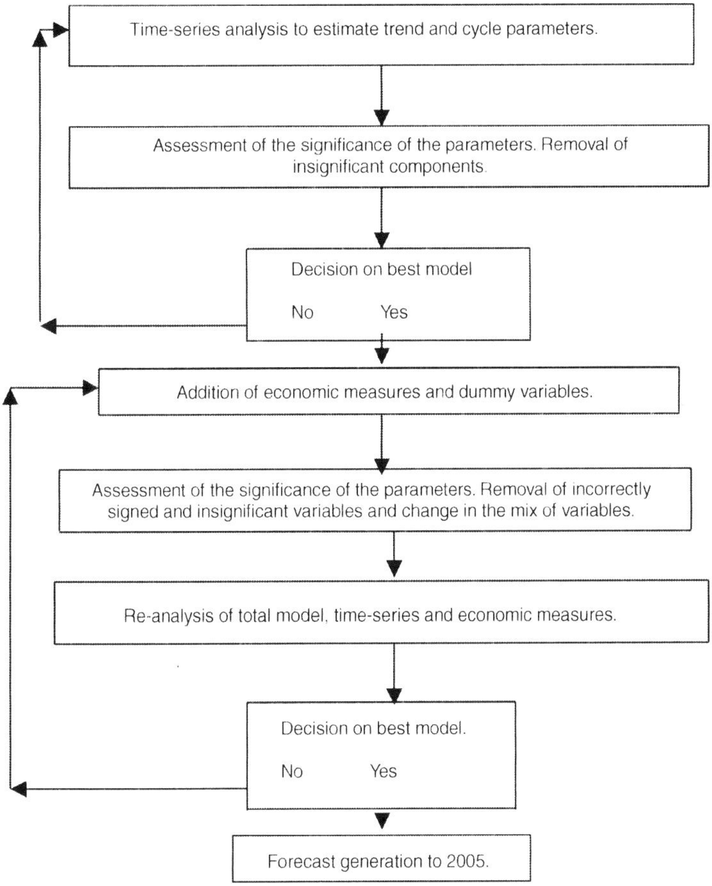

account for special economic, social and political influences that cause changes in the series. The decision to keep or remove each additional variable is based upon the variable having the "correct" sign according to economic theory and being statistically significant at the 5% level.

Because the process has the potential to include a large number of parameters in any one model, the number of economic variables added is limited to three and dummy variables to two, and no more than two cycles are interpreted initially in the series. These restrictions stop any model from becoming over-parameterized, which could lead to questionable results or simply no model solution occurring. Additionally, from a theoretical point of view it is possible to limit the number of independent variables, because previous research has clearly defined the most important economic measures influencing tourist arrivals; these are origin country income (per capita personal disposable income where available, per capita GDP otherwise), destination price (origin country-destination country exchange rate multiplied by destination CPI divided by origin CPI) and origin-destination airfares. The data sources are the China National Tourism Administration (tourist arrivals), the DX Econ database (income, prices, exchange rates) and the ABC/OAG World Airways Guide (airfares).

In some cases no economic measure was found to be significant, and the forecast process reverts to a pure time-series model. Occasionally, only a dummy variable is significant and the forecast process then reverts to a pure time-series model with one or two dummy variables. The economic measures were forecast separately using time-series methods. The forecasting process is iterative (refer to Figure 1) in that different combinations of economic and dummy variables are possible, and an iterative decision process based on statistical measures of fit is required to reach a decision on the best model.

Table 1 shows that total arrivals are projected to increase from 8.4 million in 1999 to 9.8 million in 2001, 10.5 million in 2002 and 12.3 million in 2005. The overall average annual growth rate for the Asia Pacific region is 4.3%. Countries that exhibit high average annual growth rates over the period are Japan (8.2%), South Korea (8.3%), Thailand (11.0%) and Vietnam (13.5%), but the highest average annual growth rate is projected for India (24.7%). India is now the sleeping outbound tourism giant of the Asia Pacific region, with a total population expected soon to grow beyond China's, and with a very significant middle class possessing the means to travel.

European arrivals are forecast to increase on average by 8.7% per annum over the period 1999-2005, with the highest growth rates recorded for Germany (9.0%), Sweden (9.4%), France (11.2%), Italy (13.7%) and the Netherlands (21.9%). The Americas show somewhat slower average annual growth than Europe at 8.3%. Canada is projected to grow more rapidly (14.0%) than the USA (6.7%), but the USA is forecast to remain the third largest market, after Japan and South Korea. These three largest origin markets are each forecast to generate in excess of a million tourist arrivals in China by 2005. The only origin countries that are forecast to exhibit declines in arrivals in China are Indonesia (2001) and North Korea (2001).

The main constraint upon achieving the predicted arrival volumes is air transport, and, in particular, the capacity of the non-mainland Chinese airlines which tend to be preferred by western tourists.

Regional forecasts of foreign tourist arrivals are given in Table 2. These forecasts are generated through fitting trend and cyclical components to the data series. Economic influences are not taken into account separately. The total numbers of foreign arrivals by region are greater than the totals for China as a whole because tourists often visit more than one region on a given trip. However, the number of regions visited is declining. Beijing is forecast to remain the most frequently visited region in 2005, followed by Guangdong, Jiangsu, Shanghai and Yunnan. The regions forecast to be the least visited by foreign tourists in 2005 are Qinghai and Ningxia.

The variation in the average annual growth rate is marked, with 12 regions projected to achieve positive double digit growth rates, and four regions projected to record declines in international tourist arrivals. The rate of growth also varies considerably over the period to 2005, with some regions such as Guangxi and Hainan declining in the short term and then growing. In addition, it is necessary to take into account the base number from which the growth rate is calculated; for example, there is a large increase for Ningxia (20.0%), but this is from a very small base, whereas the increase for Jiangsu (17.0%) is off a much higher base number, and is therefore much more significant in volume terms.

CONCLUDING REMARKS

The Chinese economy has grown rapidly since China started the economic reforms in 1978. The reform-induced economic growth has also led to rapid development of the tourism sector, with international tourist arrivals and international tourism receipts increasing dramatically.

TABLE 2. Forecast International Tourist Arrivals in China by Destination Region 2001-2005

Region	1999 Actual	2001	2002	2005	AAGR%
Beijing	2050200	2147700	2237100	2528100	3.9
Tianjin	281500	358350	401310	563650	16.7
Hebei	322200	393700	437980	603010	14.5
Shanxi	101100	126490	141440	197780	15.9
I.Mongolia	363500	419950	446440	526100	7.5
Liaoning	386300	509720	587390	898880	22.1
Jilin	141100	102540	91796	95864	5.3
Heilonguan	360600	502840	584270	916540	25.7
Shanghai	1287300	1328400	1358600	1453600	2.2
Jiangsu	804400	1011800	1138700	1623500	17.0
Zhejiang	506700	534760	563480	659250	5.0
Anhui	138300	150840	166070	221620	10.0
Fujian	353000	415260	448690	566020	10.1
Jiangxi	41000	49260	55932	81876	16.6
Shandong	417900	448060	471730	550520	5.3
Henan	160300	200620	223330	308050	15.4
Hubei	223300	191900	197800	201430	−1.6
Hunan	134800	137850	139400	144160	1.2
Guangdong	1487700	1618100	1706300	2001100	5.8
Guangxi	370700	335190	335370	335880	−1.6
Hainan	73200	61701	63450	85791	2.9
Chonggoing	133600	141260	145210	157750	2.9
Sichuan	179500	200940	212630	251930	6.7
Guizhou	65700	64700	65453	99852	8.7
Yunnan	725000	921070	928260	1148590	9.7
Tibet	92600	110970	121490	159410	12.0
Shaonxi	501600	525510	551990	639690	4.6
Gensu	94600	94557	98953	113410	3.3
Qinghai	8900	7493	6875	5310	−6.7
Ningxia	4500	5758	6595	9909	20.0
Xinjiang	190200	197300	207610	241890	4.5
Total	12001300	13314589	14141644	17390462	7.5

Note: AAGR denotes average annual growth rate.

Forecasts of inbound tourism from China's main source markets over the next few years show that the high overall growth rates are expected to continue, but with considerable variation from market to market. Furthermore, forecasts of international tourist arrivals in the various regions of China also exhibit markedly different growth rates.

The success of the newly developed SITEA model will need to be judged in the future by its ability to generate accurate forecasts. As the actual data on tourist arrivals in China for 2002 (and later 2005) becomes available the forecasting performance of the SITEA model can be assessed and compared with the accuracy of other models used to forecast tourism demand.

REFERENCES

Chai, J.C.H. (1998). *Transition to a Market Economy*. Oxford: Oxford University Press.

China National Tourism Administration (1999). *The Yearbook of China Tourism Statistics*. Beijing: Tourism Press of China.

Turner, L.W., & Witt, S. F. (2000). *Asia Pacific Tourism Forecasts 2000-2004*. London: Travel and Tourism Intelligence.

World Tourism Organization (1999). *Compendium of Tourism Statistics 1993-1997*. Madrid: WTO.

Yeh, K. C. (1984). Macroeconomic Changes in the Chinese Economy during the Readjustment. *China Quarterly*, 100, 691-716.

Zhang, H. Q., Chong, K., & Ap, J. (1999). An Analysis of Tourism Policy Development in Modern China. *Tourism Management*, 20, 471-485.

Learning and Ability to Pay: Developing a Model to Forecast Ski Tourism

Geoff L. Riddington

SUMMARY. The decision whether to use time series or econometric methods to forecast demand is not clear. The literature reviewed only indicates that models should be simple and ideally be able to evolve over time. In 1997 two models were proposed to forecast the numbers from Britain skiing in Europe. The first used a learning curve approach and forecast a stationary market, whilst the second used a Varying Coefficient Model linking sales and ability to pay and forecast a gradually expanding market. This paper reviews the outcomes 1996-2000, the forecast performance of the two models and the stability of the structure of both when updated. It unequivocally suggests that the learning curve approach produced better forecasts. In the penultimate section a model that attempts to combine both approaches is developed. In this context the role of "historic" data is discussed. The paper concludes that the best forecasting approach will depend upon whether the market is stable and that the weight given to data must reflect the information content of that data. *[Article copies available for a fee from The Haworth Document Delivery Service: 1-800-HAWORTH. E-mail address: <getinfo@haworthpressinc.com> Website: <http://www. HaworthPress. com> © 2002 by The Haworth Press, Inc. All rights reserved.]*

Geoff L. Riddington is Reader in Economics, Division of Economics and Enterprise, Caledonian Business School, Glasgow Caledonian University, Glasgow, UK.

Address correspondence to: Geoff L. Riddington, Division of Economics and Enterprise, Caledonian Business School, Glasgow Caledonian University, Cowcaddens, Glasgow, G4 0BA, U.K.

[Haworth co-indexing entry note]: "Learning and Ability to Pay: Developing a Model to Forecast Ski Tourism." Riddington, Geoff L. Co-published simultaneously in *Journal of Travel & Tourism Marketing* (The Haworth Hospitality Press, an imprint of The Haworth Press, Inc.) Vol. 13, No. 1/2, 2002, pp. 111-126; and: *Tourism Forecasting and Marketing* (ed: Kevin K. F. Wong and Haiyan Song) The Haworth Hospitality Press, an imprint of The Haworth Press, Inc., 2002, pp. 111-126. Single or multiple copies of this article are available for a fee from The Haworth Document Delivery Service [1-800-HAWORTH, 9:00 a.m. - 5:00 p.m. (EST). E-mail address: getinfo@haworthpressinc.com].

KEYWORDS. Forecasting, skiing, learning curve, varying coefficients

INTRODUCTION

Quantitative forecasting methods can broadly be grouped into two groups; Time Series and Econometric/Regression. In simple terms where the only information that is relevant is contained within a series then a time series approach is appropriate. However where external/environmental factors have a significant influence then it seems sensible to try to establish their precise effect and allow for changes in them in any forecast. Again, very broadly, since the economic and social environment is more likely to change in the medium or long term then econometric methods would appear "better" in these circumstances.

THE GENERAL FORECASTING PERFORMANCE OF ECONOMETRIC MODELS

A particular problem in practice is that traditional econometric models do not forecast well. Tourism demand forecasting using econometric methods has a particularly poor record (Witt and Witt (1995)). Song and Witt (2000) summarize the position thus:

"Another serious problem with traditional tourism demand models is that the forecasting performance of these models has been poor in comparison with alternative specifications; in particular they cannot even compete with the simplest time series models such as the naïve no-change model" (Song and Witt (2000) p. 26).

Econometric methodology, however, has moved forward substantially. In particular an approach strongly advocated by David Hendry amongst others and given substance in the package PCGive see Hendry and Doornick (1999) utilizes a general to specific methodology, co-integration, stationary series and error correction model specifications. Promises of improvement, however, have not been met in practice. Gonzalez and Moral (1995) for example develop a state space model with stochastic trends, evolving seasonals and the necessary co-integrated variables. To the obvious frustration of the authors in ex post analysis this sophisticated econometric approach failed to beat a time series specification. Kulendra and King (1997) had a similar experience when their error correction model of international tourist flows failed to improve over an ARIMA model. They queried the foundations of the approach; the Unit Root tests of co-integration.

Such results are not uncommon in the general econometric world. Some time ago the author carried out a comparative analysis of forecasts from the relatively sophisticated model of the consumption function by Pesaran and Evans (1986) and from a simple two variable linear model. To some dismay this suggested that, despite far superior fit the econometrically sophisticated model was inferior in terms of forecast.

Recently Clements and Hendry (1995, 1998a 1998b) have analyzed the reasons why econometric models do not perform well. Their analysis focuses on the underlying requirement of structural stability and suggests as yet unproven statistical methods for identifying and allowing for these shifts. Importantly they reject Time Varying Parameter Models, where parameter change is viewed as a steadily evolving process on the grounds that these too imply a structural stability that cannot respond well to structural breaks. Riddington (1993) looked at over 20 comparative studies of forecasts from Fixed and Varying coefficients and found improvement in every single case. More recently in the tourism area Song and Witt (2000) and Riddington (1999) also showed improvements using a TVP model specification. Thus, whilst imperfect, the current evidence strongly supports the use of varying parameters, *if an econometric specification is to be used.*

MIXED TIME SERIES AND ECONOMETRIC MODELS

In contrast to "pure" econometric models, many developments utilize time series approaches. These can take the form of "adding" explanatory variables (transform Variables) to basic time series models such as ARIMA. In tourism, for example, Garcia-Ferrer and Queralt (1997) and Young and Pedregal (1997) re-examined the model of Gonzalez and Moral (1995). Garcia-Ferrer and Queralt tested the hypothesis that the Demand for Spanish Tourism was better modelled in State Space format with varying trend and seasonal components and fixed effects from relative prices and incomes. Disturbingly they could find no evidence of significant improvement from adding the economic factors.

Young and Pedregal suggested that one of the major problems of the Gonzalez and Moral model was the uncritical application of sophisticated software and ex post analysis when the problem to be solved was undefined. The view that "forecasting" and "explanatory" models are and should be significantly different in structure is widely held. In this view ex post analysis for a forecasting model is invalid, ex ante being the only sensible approach. Thus even if, as in this case, certain specifications yield significant estimates of economic effects, they should only be used in a model if they offer significant improvement in forecasts where the values of the independents are uncertain.

The VAR model is a similar mix of econometric and time series. Recognizing the impact of collinearity, in its "purest" form no constraints are imposed on coefficients and no tests are made of significance. The VAR in this form is simply for forecasting and has to be judged on this basis alone. It carries no explanatory power.

In practice the VAR framework has been used to develop multi-equation models of whole systems. Johansen's method of identifying co-integrating vectors is central to the selection of variables along with information criteria and standard t tests. Song and Witt (2000) provide an excellent example in the tourist sector.

The limited evidence to date is that this approach combine most of the deficiencies of time series approaches with most of the deficiencies of econometric modelling, i.e., it produces a model that is complex, offers little explanation and forecasts poorly.

LEARNING CURVES

Time series models relate sales at time t to sales in previous periods $t - 1, t - 2 \ldots$. They may be written either as an autoregressive function or as a function of time e.g. the simple linear model is either written as $y_t = a + b * t$ or $y_t = y_{t-1} + b$. In general time series models have no economic interpretation, e.g., an ARIMA(3,1,1) is simply the reproduction of a data pattern identified using techniques developed by Box and Jenkins.

In contrast the Learning Curve model is derived from concepts of diffusion; the more that people come in contact with something (a product, idea, disease or technology) the more likely they are to adopt or catch it. This suggests that the rate of adoption will be exponential, assuming that there are no limits. Of course there are limits, and as the numbers who have adopted a product approach this limit it becomes harder and harder to obtain additional sales. This second half therefore suggests an adoption rate best modelled by the inverse of the exponential. The resulting "S shaped" curve may be represented algebraically by a number of functions such as the cumulative normal, cumulative lognormal (logistic), cumulative Weibull and Gompertz. Figure 1 shows three such curves derived from a Logistic.

The parameters a and b in the function are important in defining the rate of adoption and the current position in the adoption cycle. For example in the logistic the underlying rate of spread is given by *b* a whilst a large value of *a* locates t = 0 as early in the cycle (as *a* = > ∞, Adoption = > 0).

It must be emphasized that these curves represent adoption and are ideally suited to "single" purchases such as consumer durables. In this case the first derivative gives the sales, as all sales are effectively new sales. For a product such as a new destination or activity it can represent individuals who have "tried" a product, and the first derivative in this case represents sales to customers who have not previously tried the product. For total sales we need to include these sales together with repeat purchasers.

Most learning curve models have concerned either purchase of durables or the diffusion of operational practices and technology such as time to assemble goods. Surprisingly, given that the tourist industry

FIGURE 1. A Family of Logistic Curves: Sales = 100/(1 + exp(a − b * t))

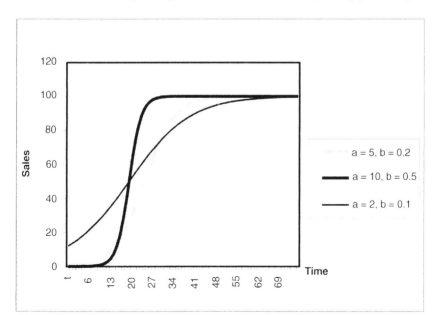

is always creating new products or marketing new destinations Learning Curve approaches do not feature in the literature.

The original new product model of Bass (1969) has been extended to include repeat purchases (e.g., Kamakura and Balasubramanian (1987)) and to model the effects of economic factors such as price and income. Kalish and Sen (1986) and Mahajan et al. (1990) provide comprehensive reviews of the literature.

A key question that has arisen is the stability of the parameters of the learning curve model. Putsis (1998), in an important paper, develops time varying parameter versions of the models of Bass (1969), Easingwood et al. (1983), Horsky (1990) and Kamakura and Balasubramanian (1987) which were then estimated by Non linear least squares, the Kalman Filter and the procedure developed by Cooley and Prescott. This work clearly demonstrates that assumptions of parameter stability in learning curve models are likely to be no more valid than those same assumptions in econometric models. Unfortunately it does not attempt to evaluate these more complex models in terms of forecast performance.

Golder and Tellis (1998) suggest a model that they term an "affordability" model. It is indistinguishable from an econometric model except for the inclusion of a Market Presence variable, which places it partially in the learning curve category. Ex ante forecasts from the model were compared with those from the simple Bass model and the model of Jain and Rao (1990). The results showed that although the model fitted less well the parameters were more stable over time and forecasts were superior on virtually all criteria.

By way of comparison Bottomley and Fildes (1998) examined a family of models (12) for five products where price affected either the rate of adoption or the total size of the market (or had no effect). Forecasts covered a range of horizons and evaluation criteria. The remarkable and rather depressing outcome was that the simplest model (Bass) was the "best," confirming the well known results of the M competitions that *simple models are often superior to theoretically more satisfying complex alternatives.*

MODELS OF SKI DEMAND

Riddington (1999) proposed two models to explain and forecast the growth and rapid decline of the ski market from the UK to Europe. The first was based on a Learning Curve Model which essentially combined a forecast of new entrants based on a saturation level and rate of growth to be estimated and a forecast of re-orders based on an unknown fraction of those who had experienced skiing in Europe.

The second model reflected the widely held view that the growth of tourism in Europe in general, and ski tourism in particular, largely reflected the growth of disposable incomes. The collapse in ski demand however preceded the decline in GNP. This collapse was explained by the specific impact of interest rates and rapidly increasing house prices on the discretionary income of the target ski market, the 18-30 year olds. The slow recovery rate was modelled on the basis that the attitude to debt changed as a result of the problems of this period (specifically Negative Equity). The forecast was however of a slower but positive growth.

DATA

The data utilized was obtained from the Monthly returns of the Civil Aviation Authority (CAA) now available at *www.caaerg.co.uk*. It was assumed that the number of passengers on Charter services to the ski airports were an accurate reflection of the total numbers of ski tourists. There were some problems relating to the change in both source and destination airports used and in the 1995 paper the decision was taken to restrict the data to "major" routes that were consistently recorded. The substantial improvement in data coverage coupled with the growth in flights from provincial airports and to new airports, particularly Turin and Toulouse, has allowed fuller reporting. For the years 1973-77 the full data is not available and the partial data has been scaled up.

THE LEARNING CURVE MODEL

The learning curve model was based on the concept of two markets. The first market consists of all those who have experienced skiing of whom an unknown percentage "repeat buy." This re-order level is assumed to be a constant δ. In this paper it is assumed that the stock of skiers in 1973 is an unknown: ST.

The second market is the market for new skiers and is derived from a learning curve based upon unknown parameters; the saturation level S and two parameters γ and β that determine the rate of growth at any time t.

These parameters determine where in the cycle the data starts and reconciles different measures of time (i.e., 1,2,3, ... or 1973, 1974, 1975, ... or 73, 74, 75 ...).

The number who have tried skiing is given by	$Y_t = S/(1 + \gamma St^{\beta})$
and new skiers by	$N_t = Y_t - Y_{t-1}$
Putting these together we obtain	$Q_t = ST + \delta(Y_t) + N_t.$

Estimation is straightforward, simply a case of an iterative search for the values of S, ST, d, b and g that minimize either Mean Absolute Error or Mean Square Error.

RESULTS FROM THE LEARNING MODEL

Figure 2 shows the fit and forecasts from a model based on the data to 1973, the fit from a model based on the whole data set, and the basic data.

The stability of the model with new data is reassuring and the overall fit satisfactory with an R-Squared value of 95%. The saturation level is estimated at 4.24 million (around 8% of the population) which corre-

FIGURE 2. Fit and Forecasts (All Data)

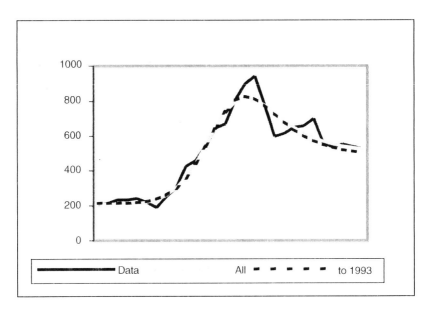

sponds quite closely to the percentage of Scots who ski in Scotland (see Riddington et al. (1998)).

The major problem appears to be that the model underestimates the initial peak, the subsequent drop and then the recovery. In the original paper it was hypothesized that the peak and subsequent collapse were the result of a significant change in availability of disposable funds, including credit, coupled with a changing attitude towards debt. In simple terms young upwardly mobile high earners, a core group of potential skiers, were both earning and borrowing at record levels in the late eighties. One result was skyrocketing property prices (another being record skier levels) but as interest rates shot up to counter inflation discretionary income, house prices and skier numbers all collapsed. The effect of negative equity was to depress the market further.

The return of confidence appears to have led in turn to an above expected boost in the skier market. This "economic" explanation led to the second model which we now examine.

RESULTS FROM THE ECONOMETRIC MODEL

The econometric model was based on a linear relationship between real money and passengers and had the form:

$$Q_t = \alpha + \beta_t{}^* \Delta M4_t + \gamma^* T + \varepsilon_t$$

$$\beta_t = \beta_{t-1} + \delta + \omega_t$$

where

- Q_t is the number of skiers per annum in thousands
- $\Delta M4_t$ is the change in Broad Money in 1982 prices in £bn
- T is the time period 1973 = 0
- δ is a constant and ω_t is zero mean normally distributed system noise.

In the 1999 paper a number of economic and demographic variables were examined both individually and in combination. Clearly, in theory, the key determinant of spend is the income and GDP is the obvious candidate. In reality the relationship was unstable and apparently insignificant.

Individuals do not treat all expenditures alike. Some items such as housing and food are best based on some smoothed "permanent" income level. Some, such as health service payments may actually be inversely related to GDP. Some (furniture) importantly will be based on the confidence of the individuals and the willingness to run up debt. High tourist spend occurs when individuals either have significant discretionary income (income after housing, food, taxes, etc.) or high levels of confidence in the economic future that they will borrow or dis-save. The building society payouts, for example had a more than proportionate effect on the tourist industry.

In this context it is important to note that the massive decline in the ski industry (and presumably in the tourist industry as a whole) preceeded the decline in the GDP. Examination of debt showed massive rises in the year before the collapse, as a result of the housing boom and consequent hyper inflation of property prices in the South East of England. The subsequent significant rises in interest rates (tightening of M4) significantly reduced the discretionary income available for leisure and recreation, leading to the collapse in ski demand over a year before the downturn in the GDP.

It was hypothesized that income available for skiing was best proxied not by GDP but a combination of growth in M4 (as credit conditions have a direct and important effect on this group of young, highly indebted individuals) and an underlying trend increase in prosperity. Given that the effect could vary and one basic objective of the paper is to examine the performance of the model it was decided to retain M4 as the key economic indicator. However for this paper it was found that "time" was actually a proxy for overall prosperity which could more sensibly be reflected by the level of real M4. Consequently the revised model has the form:

$$Q_t = \alpha + \beta_\tau{}^* \Delta M4_t + \gamma^* M4 + \varepsilon_\tau$$

$$\beta_t = \beta_{t-1} + \delta + \omega_t.$$

All the variables are significant at the 5% level and the Corrected R-Squared is 88.6%. Figure 3 shows the actual and fitted values.

A significant feature of the model is the rapidly declining influence of growth in incomes. It appears from the model that a key feature of demand in the early stages is the feeling of prosperity. In these circumstances consumers appear to be willing to try new products such as skiing. The lack of a corresponding surge post-1994 may be the result of decreased confidence (the memory of negative equity) or alternatively (or additionally) as the product reaches maturity the impact of unexpected incomes reduces until it becomes irrelevant.

FIGURE 3. VC Model with M4

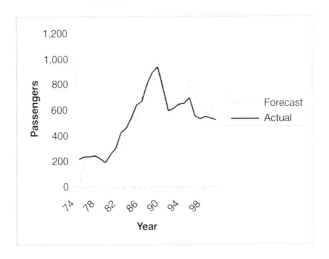

Such behavior has a parallel in investment. When there are boom conditions and high expectations, individuals appear willing to try new ventures. This magnifies the investment cycle and conversely exaggerates the recession when it eventually occurs. The next section examines how we can incorporate this effect into our learning curve model.

THE MIXED MODEL

The basic assumption is that, if an individual is feeling prosperous than they are more likely to make unusual purchases, e.g., purchase new technology items such as DVD players or new, more expensive, holiday destinations. A measure of prosperity is the liquidity of the individual, which is best represented by M4, money in circulation and credit availability. It is possible to supplement a basic model by adding a term reflecting economic conditions. In this example a Logistic Learning Curve model of similar form to the earlier model $Y_t = 1/(a + br^t)$ is used, where Y_t is the number who have tried skiing. In this form the Saturation level S is given by $1/a$, and new entrants N_t defined by dY/dt.

However if $Y_t^{-1} = \alpha + br^t$ *then* $-Y_t^{-2} \dfrac{dY}{dt} = b\ln(r).r^t$

$$i.e. N_t = \frac{dY}{dt} = Y_t^2 b \ln(r) r^t$$

The second model supplements the learning curve effect by an economic effect:

$$N_t^* = N_t + \alpha \Delta M 4$$

In addition it was thought that, since demand is constrained by supply of charter seats and these are likely to be based on demand in the previous year then demand lagged one period could also add significantly to the explanation. The parameter of this factor is β and the learning model plus these two factors is termed Model 3. For comparison purposes Model 4 consists solely of these two factors. Estimates of the four models are given in Table 1.

The unsurprising and disappointing outcome is that the addition of the economic factors is extremely marginal, indeed in terms of R-Bar squared the explanation is actually reduced by adding the supply constraint parameter.

Examination of the difference between the supplemented and basic model shows that the economic factors result in a better fit at the peak and subsequent slump. However, they also generate problems earlier in the data. A tentative conclusion is that as the product reaches maturity then the effects of economic factors becomes more important. Table 2 looks at the fit from 1987 both from the original model and from the models re-estimated from 1987 on.

TABLE 1. Parameter Values and Fit

	Model 1	Model 2	Model 3	Model 4
Start	2.12817244	1.388559	1.430332	0.20293
A	0.024072235	0.024458	0.024825	
B	41.00096926	29.33021	33.40699	
R	0.615271356	0.630623	0.625474	
R	0.080978785	0.091526	0.092165	
α		0.053412	0.051319	0.93507
β			0.000566	0.05608
R-Squared	95.15%	95.65%	95.66%	91.28%
RbarSq	94.31%	94.66%	94.41%	90.58%

This table confirms that economic factors become much more significant in the mature product years. The fit of the relatively crude Model 4 is not only dramatically improved after re-estimation but is starting to approach that of the basic Model 1, with the supplemented model 2 clearly the "best" both on an original and re-estimated basis.

This analysis however, leaves open the question of whether it is the original or re-estimated models that are likely to generate the best forecasts.

COMPARATIVE FORECASTS

Figure 4 shows the forecasts to 2010 from the original and re-estimated basic and supplemented models, using the mean change in M4 1995-2000.

Most of the forecasts are similar in projecting a steady state at around 550,000 passengers. Of course if there were significant growth, or a recession, the supplemented model would generate different forecasts. The "elasticity" of q with respect to DM4 is however extremely small at 0.11.

The exception to the steady state projection is the supplemented model re-estimated, which suggests a 20% decline over the next 10 years to 450,000. Again recession or above average growth would modify (or extend) this trend. This model may reflect the use of more relevant data or this data may simply be more "unusual" giving misleading estimates. It is the essence of forecasting that only time will tell.

CONCLUSIONS

This paper is concerned with the development of a model to forecast skiing. The literature suggests that the best forecasting model is

TABLE 2. The Fit of Models Post-1987

	Model 1	Model 2	Model 3	Model 4
Post-1987 Fit				
Rsquared	81.00%	85.60%	85.79%	67.35%
RBarSq	75.31%	79.20%	76.91%	61.41%
Post-1987 Fit (Re-Estimated Model)				
Rsquared	85.03%	90.14%	90.18%	81.38%
RBarSq	80.53%	85.76%	84.05%	77.99%

FIGURE 4. Forecasts to 2010

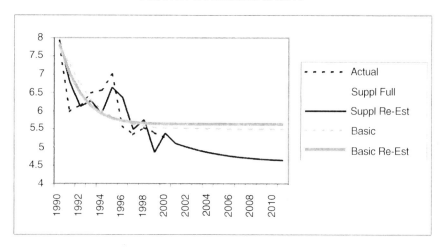

likely to be simple but flexible and, given that, the combination of autoregressive and economic factors can produce reasonable models. The paper then reviews forecasts made in 1997 from two radically different models of demand for ski charters form the UK. It found that the "learning curve model" was significantly better but nevertheless underestimated the variance that actually occurred. When the series was modelled using post 1987 data, it became clear that some economic information added significantly to the basic learning curve model. It is suggested that this is probably the best model at the present time, but as the market matures further economic information may well become dominant.

The use of all available data is rarely questioned. However, the information conveyed by the data declines the older it becomes to a level where it may be totally misleading. The logic is that perhaps all models should be specified in a varying coefficient form. This study suggests that not only should we consider different models for new and mature products but that we should perhaps separate the data for the two periods. The test of this supposition will be the actual demand over the next few years. If the market declines as projected in the re-estimated supplemented model then we can probably conclude that the earlier data would simply have distorted the "true" estimates of the model at the current time.

Finally it is important to note that this "update" paper is very unusual. Few authors return and re-examine their forecasts and the arguments they then presented; it is a task fraught with danger and far less satisfying than building a new model using the latest methodologies and an array of possible variables. It is believed, however, that this is an important way to progress. The evidence suggests econometric and time series model building has become subject to massive diminishing marginal returns; more complex, less understandable and often more inaccurate in terms of forecasts. The alternative is to look back in depth at what has been done, how well it has worked and where it has gone wrong.

REFERENCES

Bain A.D. (1964) *The Growth in Television Ownership in the United Kingdom.* Cambridge University Press.

Bass F.M. (1969) A new product growth model for consumer durables. *Management Science*, 15, 215-227.

Bottomley P. and Fildes R. (1998) Prices in Models of Innovation Diffusion. *Journal of Forecasting* 17, 539-555.

Clements M. and Hendry D. (1995) Intercept Corrections and Structural Change. *Journal of Applied Econometrics*, 11, 475-494.

Clements M. and Hendry D. (1998a) Forecasting Economic Processes. *International Journal of Forecasting*, 11, 111-131.

Clements M. and Hendry D. (1998b) *Forecasting Economic Time Series.* Cambridge University Press.

Easingwood C. Mahajan V. and Muller E. (1983) A nonuniform influence innovation diffusion model of new product acceptance. *Marketing Science*, 2, 273-295.

Garcia-Ferrer and Queralt (1997) A note on forecasting international tourism demand in Spain. *International Journal of Forecasting*, 13, 539-549.

Golder P. and Tellis G (1998) Beyond Diffusion: An Affordability Model of the Growth of New Consumer Durables. *Journal of Forecasting*, 17, 167-346.

Gonzalez P. and Moral P. (1995) An analysis of the international tourism demand in Spain. *International Journal of Forecasting*, 11, 233-251.

Hendry D. and Doornick J (1999) *Empirical Modelling using PCGive.* Timberlake Consultants Press.

Horsky D. (1990) The effects of income, price and information on the diffusion of new consumer durables. *Marketing Science*, 9, 342-365.

Jain D. and Rao R. (1990). Effect of Price and Demand for durables: modeling, estimation and findings. *Journal of Business Economics and Statistics*, 8, 163-170.

Kalish S. and Sen S. (1986) Diffusion Modes and the marketing mix for single products in Mahajan V. and Wind Y (eds) *Innovation Diffusion Models of New Product Acceptance.* Ballinger, 87-115.

Kamakura W. and Balasubramanian S. (1987) Long term forecasting with innovation diffusion models: the impact of replacement purchases. *Journal of Forecasting*, 6, 1-20.

Kulendra N. and King M. (1997) Forecasting International Tourist Flows using Error Correction and Time Series Models. *International Journal of Forecasting*, 13, 319-327.

Mahajan V. Muller E. and Bass F. (1990) New product diffusion models in marketing: a review and directions for research. *Journal of Marketing*, 54, 1-26.

Pesaran M. and Evans R.(1984) Inflation, Capital Gains, and U.K. Personal Savings: 1953-1981. *Economic Journal*, 94, 237-57.

Putsis W. (1998) Parameter Variation and New Product Diffusion. *Journal of Forecasting*, 17, 231-257.

Riddington (1993) Time Varying Coefficient Models and their Forecasting Performance. *Omega: The International Journal of Management Science* 21, 573-585.

Riddington G. (1999) Forecasting Ski Demand: Comparing Learning Curve and Varying Parameter Coefficient Approaches. *Journal of Forecasting*, 18, 205-214.

Riddington G. Radford A. and Milne N. (1998) The Economic Impact of Scottish Ski Centres on the HIE Region. *Fraser of Allendar Quarterly Review*. 23(2), 48-55.

Song H., Romilly P. and Liu X. (1999) An empirical study of UK Outbound Tourism. *Applied Economics*, 32, 611-625.

Song H. and Witt S.F. (2000) *Tourism Demand Modelling and Forecasting: Modern Econometric Approaches*. Pergamon Press.

Witt S.F. and Witt D.A. (1995) Forecasting Tourist Demand: A Review of Empirical Research. *International Journal of Forecasting*, 11, 447-75.

Young and Pedregal (1997) Comments on "An analysis of the international tourism demand in Spain" by P. Gonzalez and P. Moral. *International Journal of Forecasting*, 13, 551-556.

Forecasting Travel Patterns
Using Palmore's Cohort Analysis

Lori Pennington-Gray
Deborah L. Kerstetter
Rod Warnick

SUMMARY. The purpose of this study was to introduce Palmore's (1978) method of cohort analysis and illustrate its potential application to tourism forecasting. Results suggested that (a) older cohorts participate less frequently in international travel than younger cohorts, (b) decrease in participation continues as one ages, and (c) changes in travel behavior are due primarily to period effects. With respect to the impact these findings may have on the tourism industry, the results suggest that marketers should monitor the aggregate changes taking place within targeted cohorts, and strategic planning should not be based on an assessment of differences between cohorts at one point in time. *[Article copies available for a fee from The Haworth Document Delivery Service: 1-800-HAWORTH. E-mail address: <getinfo@haworthpressinc.com> Website: <http://www.HaworthPress.com> © 2002 by The Haworth Press, Inc. All rights reserved.]*

KEYWORDS. Cohort analysis, travel, forecasting

Lori Pennington-Gray is Assistant Professor in Recreation, Parks and Tourism, University of Florida. Deborah L. Kerstetter is Associate Professor in Leisure Studies, Penn State University. Rod Warnick is Professor in Hotel, Restaurant and Travel Administration Department, University of Massachusetts, Amherst.

Address correspondence to: Lori Pennington-Gray, University of Florida, Recreation, Parks and Tourism, 300 FLG, USA (E-mail: penngray@hhp.ufl.edu).

[Haworth co-indexing entry note]: "Forecasting Travel Patterns Using Palmore's Cohort Analysis." Pennington-Gray, Lori, Deborah L. Kerstetter, and Rod Warnick. Co-published simultaneously in *Journal of Travel & Tourism Marketing* (The Haworth Hospitality Press, an imprint of The Haworth Press, Inc.) Vol. 13, No. 1/2, 2002, pp. 127-145; and: *Tourism Forecasting and Marketing* (ed: Kevin K. F. Wong and Haiyan Song) The Haworth Hospitality Press, an imprint of The Haworth Press, Inc., 2002, pp. 127-145. Single or multiple copies of this article are available for a fee from The Haworth Document Delivery Service [1-800-HAWORTH, 9:00 a.m. - 5:00 p.m. (EST). E-mail address: getinfo@haworthpressinc.com].

INTRODUCTION

At the core of American history lies a remarkable pattern. ". . . Every two decades or so. . . people change how they feel about themselves, the culture, the nation, and the future" (Strauss & Howe, 1997, p. 3). This change is represented in what the Greeks referred to as "genos," and what we call a "generation." It is the "aggregate of all people born over roughly the span of a phase of life who share a common location in history and, hence, a common collective persona" (Strauss & Howe, 1997, p. 16). Due to their shared life experiences-things like music, economic conditions, world events, natural disasters, or technology, for example-members of a generation bond together.

The common life experiences that help to define generations will determine values and conduct (Gerber, Wolff, Klores, & Brown, 1989) and "exercise as much or more influence on buying and purchasing than do more commonly understood demographic factors like income, education, and gender" (Smith & Clurman, 1997, p. XVII). For example, individuals who Smith and Clurman refer to as Matures (i.e., born between 1909 and 1945) think of leisure as something that is a reward for hard work. This belief is markedly different from that of Boomers (i.e., born between 1946 and 1964) who think of leisure as *the* point in life. Given their difference in beliefs or values, it can be expected that their perceptions of and involvement with travel will also vary.

Very little research exists which documents the change in different generations' or cohorts' travel behavior over time. The term generation has been used synonymously with the term cohort because it ". . .consists of a birth cohort (or of adjacent birth cohorts) internally homogeneous in some important respect and distinctly different from persons born earlier or later" (Glenn, 1977, p. 9). A cohort is defined as "those people within a geographically or otherwise delineated population who experienced the same significant life event within a given period of time" (Glenn, 1977, p. 8). Further, the influences associated with birth cohort membership are considered to be "cohort effects" and, as such, have been the focus of various studies. For example, through an examination of cohort effects on the travel patterns of German residents, Opperman (1995) found that type of travel and destination region preferences were dependent on cohort membership. Moreover, he found that transportation usage differed by cohort groups. More recently, You and O'Leary (2000) addressed cohort effects on the travel behavior and travel philosophies of older Japanese tourists. Their results indicated that younger and older cohorts differ with respect to their level of travel activity as they age as well as their philosophies about traveling for pleasure.

In the early '90s, Warnick (1993a, 1993b) addressed the domestic travel behavior of various cohorts. Using *Simmons Market Research data*, he found that the Baby Boom Generation's participation rate in domestic travel declined at the same or a lower rate than the overall population. The Silent Generation (those 35 to 44 in 1979 and then age 45 to 54 in 1989) experienced a rise in participation rates. All other cohorts showed greater decline rates than the overall population. In conclusion, Warnick argued that documenting the travel behavior of cohorts is useful when predicting future travel trends. While the aforementioned studies provide evidence for the value of cohort analysis, they are weakened by the researchers' use of a cross-sectional approach. Such an approach is problematic because the simultaneous effects associated with aging, the influences of a birth cohort, and given periods of time are not accounted for (Singleton, Jr. & Straits, 1999). In addition, the influences of technology, political events, improved lifestyles and educational opportunities (Godbey, 1992; Schaie, 1996) are not taken into account, all of which put later born cohorts at an advantage. According to McPherson (1990), the preferences and needs of future generations of adults can only be understood by studying particular age cohorts at different stages of their lives. A recent study conducted by Pennington-Gray and Kerstetter (2001) did just that. They focused on changes over time in preferences for pleasure travel between two cohorts of older Canadian adults. However, their study was limited to two time periods. Cohort analysis involving three or more time periods will result in more robust findings.

As early as 1965, Ryder argued for the utility of the cohort as a unit of analysis in the study of social and cultural change. Little more than a decade later, recognizing the value of cohort analysis, Glenn (1977) suggested that it provides ". . . insight into the effects of human aging and into the nature of social, cultural and political change" (p. 7). In essence, cohort analysis is valuable as a tool for measuring cohorts on a given variable such as change in leisure behavior at two or more points in time (Neuman, 1997; Reynolds & Rentz, 1981).

Cohort analysis also has potential for forecasting the future travel behavior of different generations of travelers. Archer (1994) argued that forecasting is an "essential element in the process of management . . ." (p. 105). It provides data that informs allocation, strategic planning and marketing decisions within state and national tourism offices, for example (Crouch, 1994). Because forecasting is critical to effective management of tourism businesses, forecasts should be focused on patterns of groups rather than individuals because, according to Smith (1984), "large groups tend to display more stable patterns that cluster around a mean value" (p. 102). This is especially true when researchers assume that historical patterns of aggregate groups (i.e., cohorts) will continue (Young & Smith, 1979).

Lacking from the scholarly literature is empirical research on the changing preferences of cohort groups in the area of travel and tourism. Therefore, the objective of this study was to examine changes in travel preferences of six cohorts over time across one activity, international travel.

International Travel

Much of the research related to travel behavior focuses on domestic travel or, if tied to international travel, on visitors hosted by the United States. Scant attention is paid to U.S. residents who travel abroad (i.e., internationally). According to Marano (1998), in 1999 more than 57 million residents were expected to travel abroad. This volume of travel is disconcerting to federal agencies such as the International Trade Administration, within the U.S. Department of Commerce, who are concerned that travel abroad by U.S. residents will continue to impact the travel trade surplus. For example, in 1997 the travel industry in the United States produced a surplus of $25 billion. Two years later the surplus had been reduced by more than 20%. Given the impact increased travel by U.S. residents has had and may continue to have on the balance of trade between the United States and other countries, it is important to forecast what changes can be anticipated in the international travel behavior of residents.

Cohort Analysis: A Useful Method of Forecasting?

Historically, researchers have taken cross-sectional data and projected it developmentally over time (Bonnici & Fredenberger, 1992). They've mistakenly assumed that if one age group heavily consumes a product, then this trend will continue in the future. Adopting this approach has been disastrous for large, global companies such as Coca-Cola and Ford Motor Company. A useful forecasting alternative is cohort analysis (Palmore, 1978; Reynolds & Rentz, 1981). According to Riley, Johnson and Foner (1972), the ability to examine development (i.e., aging) and cohort differences simultaneously is a unique property of cohort analysis. In fact, recognizing the relationship between age and cohort, as well as period (i.e., time) effects, influences the way in which businesses address the future.

Cohort analysis has proven valuable to businesses on three fronts. First, it has been used to segment markets: Gunnerson (1986) adopted cohort analysis to identify distinct market segments. Cohort analysis has also been used to drive advertising (Exter, 1986; Wolfe, 1988). As Meredith and Schewe (1994) suggested, "cohort effects help reveal the underlying mindset toward different categories of products and services and can help make advertising aimed at specific age groups without offending those groups" (p. 22). Third, Ambry (1990) and Jansson (1989) utilized cohort analysis to forecast the needs and wants of groups. Tongren (1988), on the other hand, forecasted the use of electronic media as a source of shopping information. According to Holbrook and Schindler (1994), findings from cohort analysis can and should be used to guide the design of products and promotional stimuli.

While cohort analysis has proven to be a useful technique, being able to document the influence of age, cohort and period on individuals' future behavior is problematic. For example, it is difficult to determine which of the three variables accounts for the variation in behavior. And, interpretation is often times confusing because the effects of age, cohort and period are confounded. Palmore's (1978) triad method is one technique that emphasizes three levels of analysis in order to prevent the conceptual and operational confusion that often accompanies cohort analysis. Therefore, we used Palmore's method of cohort analysis in this study to understand international travel patterns. The following research question guided this study:

> Of the three effects (age, period and cohort), which one has the greatest influence on changes in international travel patterns over time?

METHODS

One key to the success of cohort analysis is to utilize data on participation rates and generations that has been consistently collected over time. Another key to success is comparable databases that span at least 10 years allowing the researcher to track changes over time as generations or cohorts' age. Obtaining this type of data is difficult because very few comprehensive data sets exist. However, one agency that does have such data is Simmons Market Research Bureau. The Bureau has conducted the *Study of Media and Markets* since 1979. The data set associated with the study contains sample sizes which range from 25,000 in the late '70s to approximately 35,000 in the '90s. The data is managed in groupings in a data base management program. Therefore, only mean scores for groups are available.

The sample data is projected to an adult population (those 18 years of age and older) comprised of 6 cohorts: 18 to 24, 25 to 34, 35 to 44, 45 to 54, 55 to 64, and 65 years of age and older. While these cohorts were pre-determined by Simmons Market Research Bureau, they do closely match the cohorts identified by the U.S. Census Bureau. More importantly, they meet the minimum criteria (i.e., 10 year span) for the establishment of a cohort (Foot & Stoffman, 1997; Hicks & Hicks, 1999).

Travel activities reviewed in the *Study* include, for example, domestic travel, international travel, and cruise ship vacations. For the purpose of this study, two types (i.e., vacation and personal) of international travel were analyzed. We included both types of international travel because of the way in which Simmons collects and reports the data. For example, individuals are first asked, "Have you yourself made any trips outside the United States, or to Hawaii or Alaska, in the last three years?" If they indicate, "yes," they are then asked whether each trip was made ". . . primarily for business reasons (paid by company), vacation or personal reasons?" Thus, the resulting data on international travel is reported by reason (i.e., business, vacation or personal). It is important to note that Simmons does not recognize trips to Canada or Mexico as international trips if individuals do not stay overnight. Further, travel for military purposes while serving in the military is also discounted.

DATA ANALYSIS

Three levels of analysis were conducted to examine changes in international vacation and international personal travel: (1) computing observable differences; (2) inferring which effects (i.e., age, cohort, period) produced the observable differences; and (3) imputing causes. Observable differences include: (1) longitudinal differences-those between early and later measurements on the same cohort, (2) cross sectional differences-those between younger and older cohorts (and age groups) at one point in time, and (3) time-lag differences-those between an older cohort at an earlier measurement and a younger cohort at a later measurement (Figure 1). Calculating these differences assists in identifying whether the cohort, age and period effects are linearly dependent. Although cohort analysis cannot unravel with absolute certainty which of the three effects is responsible for change, it can provide some evidence of the strength of the influence of each effect.

Addressing inferred effects, the second level of analysis is important because researchers can document which effects (i.e., age, cohort or period) best explain the observable differences (i.e., longitudinal, cross-sectional, time-lag) noted in the first level of analysis. Z-tests are used to determine inferred effects. Each observable difference is composed of two and only two effects:

- Longitudinal = age + period effects
- Cross-sectional = age + cohort effects
- Time-lag = period + cohort effects

The results of the analysis will fall into one of three categories: (1) no significant differences, (2) two significant differences, or (3) three significant differences. If there are no significant differences, no effects

FIGURE 1. Observable Differences

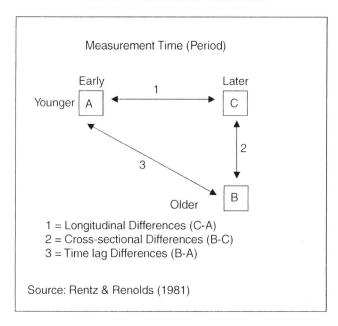

(i.e., age, cohort or period) are assumed. If two significant differences occur, a "pure" effect is assumed. The condition of three significant differences is most difficult to deal with. According to Reynolds and Rentz (1981), "one cannot separate the three effects or estimate their values unless there are other grounds for assuming that one of the effects is not present. However, where there is reason to assume that one effect is not present, one can proceed to analyze the proportion of variance of the other two" (p. 66). Although three significant differences are difficult to interpret, according to Reynolds and Rentz (1981) it can be done.

The final level of analysis is the imputing of causes. This is accomplished by running Z-tests on the differences between proportions. Z-tests were used due to the size of the sample (N = ~ 35,000). The first step in the Z-tests was calculating the standard error. Next, a triad table was created, providing the basis for the Z-tests among the three effects. Finally, Z-tests were calculated on the differences between the proportions. The magnitude of the effect is the estimated mean of the two significant effects.

FINDINGS

Observable Differences

The data (i.e., percentage of adults who've traveled internationally for vacation or personal reasons) by period of measurement and age group (see Tables 1 & 2), were used to compute observable differences (i.e., longitudinal, cross-sectional and time lag). More specifically, the differences (see Tables 3 & 4) were calculated using the triad method as seen in Figure 1. For example, the longitudinal difference for Triad 1 (-12.1%) was computed by deducting .388 from .267 (see Table 1 for this data). The cross-sectional difference (4.6%) for Triad 1, on the other hand, was computed by deducting .221 from .267. The final difference for Triad 1, time-lag (-16.7%), was computed by deducting .388 from .221.

Inferred Effects

In the second stage of analysis, we assessed which of the effects were at work. This was accomplished by referencing the number of significant differences identified through the Z-tests. According to Bonnici and Fredenberger (1991), there are three, and only three, basic patterns of ob-

TABLE 1. Participation in International "Vacation" Travel

	Average Number of Participants (Sample Size)				
Age Group	1976	1981	1986	1991	1996
18 to 24	0.388 (1,107)	0.221 (955)	0.053 (1,457)	0.097 (511)	0.152 (827)
25 to 34	0.457 (972)	0.267 (1,195)	0.076 (1,591)	0.111 (1,147)	0.148 (1,083)
35 to 44	0.445 (549)	0.263 (796)	0.081 (1,353)	0.123 (863)	0.133 (1,064)
45 to 54	0.419 (732)	0.256 (589)	0.093 (945)	0.122 (608)	0.138 (834)
55 to 64	0.368 (782)	0.228 (429)	0.088 (777)	0.131 (315)	0.149 (580)
65 and Older	0.222 (436)	0.143 (584)	0.064 (647)	0.072 (521)	0.133 (715)
Total	0.4598 (4578)	0.2754 (4548)	0.091 (6,770)	0.1312 (3,965)	0.1706 (5,103)

TABLE 2. Participation in International "Personal" Travel

	Average Number of Participants (Sample Size)				
Age Group	1976	1981	1986	1991	1996
18 to 24	0.350 (3,804)	0.201 (3,208)	0.052 (1,458)	0.020 (2,476)	0.033 (3,808)
25 to 34	0.342 (5,625)	0.191 (4,947)	0.039 (3,100)	0.026 (4,897)	0.026 (6,166)
35 to 44	0.311 (4,345)	0.178 (3,533)	0.044 (2,491)	0.023 (4,615)	0.025 (5,662)
45 to 54	0.335 (4,510)	0.189 (3,683)	0.042 (2,092)	0.024 (3,092)	0.027 (4,262)
55 to 64	0.309 (3,023)	0.172 (3,250)	0.035 (1,955)	0.015 (2,752)	0.028 (3,088)
65 and Older	0.181 (2,457)	0.103 (2,155)	0.024 (1,725)	0.018 (2,083)	0.023 (4,135)
Total	0.3656 (23,764)	0.2064 (20,776)	0.0472 (12,848)	0.0252 (19,915)	0.0324 (27,121)

servable differences: no significant differences, two significant differences and three significant differences. "It is impossible to have only one significant difference because each difference is related to the other two: one can predict any thread difference from the other two" (p. 286). If only one effect is noted, there is an error in the data and no effects are inferred. When two significant differences are present, the effects are considered to be "pure." This pure effect can be interpreted as follows:

- Longitudinal and cross-sectional differences = age effect
- Longitudinal and time-lag differences = period effect
- Cross-sectional and time-lag differences = cohort effect

Other possible explanations for two significant differences may include: (1) there are two equal and opposite effects which are reflected in

TABLE 3. Triads for International "Vacation" Travelers

Triad	Longitudinal Difference (%)	Cross-Sectional Difference (%)	Time-Lag Difference (%)
Group 1: 1976 to 1981			
1	12.1%	4.6%	−16.7%
2	19.4%	0.4%	−19.0%
3	−18.9%	−0.7%	−18.2%
4	−19.1%	−2.8%	−16.3%
5	22.5%	8.5%	−14.0%
Group 2: 1981 to 1986			
6	−14.5%	2.3%	−16.8%
7	−18.6%	0.5%	−19.1%
8	−17.0%	1.2%	−18.2%
9	−16.8%	−0.5%	−16.3%
10	−16.4%	2.4%	−14.0%
Group 3: 1986 to 1991			
11	5.8%	1.4%	4.4%
12	4.7%	1.2%	3.5%
13	4.1%	−0.1%	4.2%
14	3.8%	0.9%	2.9%
15	−1.6%	−5.9%	4.3%
Group 4: 1991 to 1996			
16	5.1%	−0.4%	5.5%
17	2.2%	−1.5%	3.7%
18	1.5%	0.5%	1.0%
19	2.7%	1.1%	1.6%
20	0.2%	−1.6%	1.8%

the two significant differences, (2) there is the possibility that there are three effects, two equal and opposite and one effect that is reflected by the significant differences. Using the principle of parsimony, Bonnici and Fredenberger (1991) opted to go with the first explanation, that the effects are "pure."

If three effects are significant, the situation is considered ambiguous because it is impossible to separate the three effects. Hence, as with the situation with one significant effect, the results are ignored (denoted by

TABLE 4. Triads for International "Personal" Travelers

Triad	Longitudinal Difference (%)	Cross-Sectional Difference (%)	Time-Lag Difference (%)
Group 1: 1976 to 1981			
1	−15.9%	−0.1%	−14.9%
2	−16.4%	−1.3%	−15.1%
3	−12.2%	1.1%	−13.3%
4	−16.3%	−1.7%	−14.6%
5	−20.6%	−6.9%	−13.7%
Group 2: 1981 to 1986			
6	−16.2%	−1.3%	−14.9%
7	14.7%	0.5%	15.2%
8	−13.6%	−0.2%	−13.4%
9	−15.4%	−0.7%	−14.7%
10	−14.8%	−1.1%	−13.7%
Group 3: 1986 to 1991			
11	−2.6%	0.6%	−3.2%
12	−1.6%	−0.3%	−1.3%
13	−2.0%	0.1%	−2.1%
14	−2.7%	−0.9%	−1.8%
15	−1.7%	0.3%	−2.0%
Group 4: 1991 to 1996			
16	0.6%	−0.7%	1.3%
17	−0.1%	−0.1%	0.0%
18	0.4%	0.2%	0.2%
19	0.4%	0.1%	0.3%
20	0.8%	−0.5%	1.3%

a dash in Tables 5 & 6). The magnitude of the effects is the estimate mean of the two significant effects.

International Vacation Travelers

Results of the triad analysis for international vacation travelers (Table 5) indicated that the most common "pure" effect is the period effect. This is noted by the overall presence of period effects across all the triads (1 to 20). More specifically, period effects were present in all four groups (i.e.,

TABLE 5. T-tests, Inferred Effects and Magnitude of Effects for International "Vacation" Travelers

Triad	Longitudinal Difference (%)	Cross-Sectional Difference (%)	Time-Lag Difference (%)	Inferred Effect (s)	Magnitude of Effect(s)
Group 1: 1976 to 1981					
1	10.10	−11.09	21.24	-	
2	115.53*	-0.62	26.11*	P	71
3	24.32	5.52	27.98	-	
4	34.70	−165.70	28.73	-	
5	17.88	85.08	12.08	-	
Group 2: 1981 to 1986					
6	9.93	5.15	16.59	-	
7	26.00*	1.53	18.30*	P	22
8	19.90*	2.85	14.27*	P	17
9	23.68	−27.43	22.40	-	
10	16.47	8.91	19.28	-	
Group 3: 1986 to 1991					
11	−10.95*	−2.14	35.52*	P	12
12	51.11*	6.85	−42.10*	P	5
13	16.25*	0.20	−17.83*	P	-1
14	37.64	3.34	−17.21	-	
15	4.42	13.27	51.98	-	
Group 4: 1991 to 1996					
16	8.60*	0.65	216.08*	P	104
17	58.96	65.46	61.43	-	
18	6.52*	1.36	7.26*	P	1
19	9.32*	2.01	6.21*	P	2
20	0.37	2.88*	88.27	C	44

A = Age effect (significant longitudinal and cross-sectional differences)
C = Cohort effect (significant cross-sectional and time-lag differences)
P = Period effect (significant longitudinal and time-lag differences)
*- significantly different from zero at α = .05 using a Z-test on the difference between proportions

1976-1981, 1981-1986, 1986-1991, 1991-1996) of triads. In addition, the number of period effects was greater for the third (i.e., 1986-1991) and fourth groups (i.e., 1991-1996) of triads. Both groups had three significant period effects. The greater the number of significant effects, the greater the strength of the period effects for that time frame.

TABLE 6. T-Tests, Inferred Effects and Magnitude of Effects for International "Personal" Travelers

Triad	Longitudinal Difference (%)	Cross-Sectional Difference (%)	Time-Lag Difference (%)	Inferred Effect(s)	Magnitude of Effect (s)
Group 1: 1976 to 1981					
1	7.09*	1.28	10.44*	P	8.77
2	9.87*	1.29	5.66*	P	7.77
3	4.75*	0.85	3.45*	P	4.10
4	27.48*	-1.77	9.60*	P	18.54
5	7.14	2.35	-201.72	-	
Group 2: 1981 to 1986					
6	3.89	2.91	4.00	-	
7	4.85*	1.53	4.53*	P	4.69
8	3.76*	0.48	3.32*	P	3.54
9	3.15	-35.15	2.99	-	
10	2.43	4.07	2.36	-	
Group 3: 1986 to 1991					
11	4.92*	-0.23	-25.66*	P	-10.37
12	-17.24*	0.46	-15.74*	P	-16.49
13	7.87*	0.57	-8.93*	P	-8.40
14	25.66*	1.84	10.80*	P	-7.43
15	4.69*	1.10	23.44*	P	-9.38
Group 4: 1991 to 1996					
16	-1.01	1.13	51.00	-	
17	-2.65*	4.38*	0.00	A	-1.33
18	1.74	0.54	-1.45	-	
19	1.38	0.18	-1.16	-	
20	-1.48	0.90	70.26	-	

A = Age effect (significant longitudinal and cross-sectional differences)
C = Cohort effect (significant cross-sectional and time-lag differences)
P = Period effect (significant longitudinal and time-lag differences)
*- significantly different from zero at $\alpha = .05$ using a Z-test on the difference between proportions

The magnitude of the effects (estimated mean of two significant effects) revealed that for international vacation travelers' period effects were greater for younger age groups. For example, in the second group of triads, triad 7 and triad 8 had period effects. Triad 9 and triad 10 did not. In addition, the magnitude of the effects was always greater for the younger cohorts. For example, in the fourth group of triads (i.e., 1991 to

1996), triad 16 had a magnitude of effects value of 104. This value was much larger than that of triad 19.

The results associated with triad 20 (Table 5) suggest that there are also cohort effects impacting individuals' participation in international vacation travel and that these cohort effects are *fairly* large in magnitude (magnitude = 44). The presence of this cohort effect does not negate period effects, rather it suggests that the increase in participation in international travel can be accounted for by cohort membership.

International Personal Travelers

Results of the triad analysis for international personal travelers indicated that the most common "pure" effect is the period effect (Table 6). Period effects were most pronounced between 1976 and 1981 (triads 1 to 5) and 1986 and 1991 (triads 11 to 15). The greater the number of significant effects, the greater the strength of the period effects for that time frame. Thus, the strength of the period effects was greatest between 1986 and 1991, followed by 1976 to 1981.

With respect to the magnitude of the effects, in general, it was greater in later time periods (refer to the magnitude of effects column in Table 6). For example, all but one of the triads in group three (i.e., 11 to 15) had magnitude levels in excess of those reported for the earlier triads (i.e., 1 to 10). This pattern indicates a cohort-period interaction, suggesting that future travel will be affected by cohort membership as well as the time period.

Finally, an examination of the differences associated with the 17th triad suggests that age effects are present. Again, the presence of age effects do not negate period effects, instead they suggest that the small decrease in participation in international personal travel (magnitude = −1.33) can be accounted for by age in that particular year.

DISCUSSION

Cohort analysis does have potential for predicting the future travel behavior of different generations of travelers. Using Palmore's triad method we were able to document observable differences between and within cohorts of international travelers and infer what effects (i.e., age, cohort and period) best explained the differences.

Some interesting patterns were noted with respect to the observable differences. For example, when examining the longitudinal and time-

n able to determine when, how and what types of shifts in demand
ld occur. They would have, for example, recognized and responded
is cohort's burgeoning interest in heritage and culture.

When examining the magnitude of the period effects, however, we
d that an interaction between period and cohort effects exists. This
ing is important because it lends support to the contention that
bers of a birth cohort can differ from each other in terms of their
re behavior (i.e., international travel). As we argued early on in this
uscript, common life experiences help to define generations of peo-
nd may impact their behavior (Gerber et al., 1989). The results of
study lend empirical support to this argument. Further, the fact that
rences between cohorts arose at various periods of time suggests
factors such as the economy (e.g., fluctuating value of the dollar,
expensive air travel); world events (e.g., the destruction of the
in Wall, the events of '9-11'); variation in the roles of family mem-
(e.g., dual income earners); etc., do have an impact on the way in
h cohorts respond to activities such as travel. Overall, then, it is
r from these study data that change in international travel will be
o a combination of period and cohort effects. Given future genera-
s' interest and participation in all kinds of travel, including eco and
nture-based travel, both of which are receiving increased attention
nd the world, there appears to be a bright future for international
l.

hat do these results suggest for the future of forecasting in travel
ourism research? Despite the success of cohort analysis evidenced
is and other studies, we should not believe that "generations" or
orts" can explain all variations in travel behavior (Smith in
eman, 1998). For example, Weiss (2000) argued that there is no
rage" type of household in the United States today. The traditional
el, married couples with children, makes up about one quarter of all
eholds. About the same percentage of Americans live alone, an in-
se of 17% since 1940. Consider what may happen if older Ameri-
become dependent on their children for care? Despite being from
ame generation, mightn't the composition of an individual's house-
and the responsibilities associated with maintaining it affect over-
isure behavior, including travel?

addition, it is expected that ethnic diversity will impact the ways in
h individuals engage in leisure activities, including travel (Archer,
). According to Barone (2001), immigrants bring with them habits
nd they developed to adapt to their home country. "These habits of
are not easily discarded; they are handed down from parents to

lag differences for international travelers we found t[...]
servable differences were consistently negative for t[...]
periods and positive for the last time period. The in[...]
older cohorts participate less frequently in internat[...]
younger cohorts and that this decrease in participation[...]
ages. However, this pattern is reversed from 1991 to 1[...]
time period); older cohorts begin participating more fr[...]
national travel than younger cohorts. Perhaps some of[...]
ing is what Baltes (1997) has referred to as selective [...]
compensation (SOC). He argued that people use mo[...]
physical and intellectual resources to design strategie[...]
cessful aging. In the context of travel, individuals ma[...]
ries of changes in order to arrive at a point in their lif[...]
adapted to their surroundings and/or changes in their[...]
to return to international travel. The fact that the obser[...]
were positive for the last time period studied, howeve[...]
plained. Perhaps it is due to an anomaly in the data [...]
cannot account for given our use of secondary data[...]
overall finding leaves us with an important question.[...]
terns still exist in another 10 to 20 years? Given St[...]
(1997) contention that people change how they feel [...]
the culture, etc., every 10-20 years, it is imperative t[...]
collect data over time if we are to truly understand ch[...]
The data we had available to us was limited to a 20[...]
Adding another 20 years to the data will allow us to [...]
or not the patterns we've seen in this data set are truly[...]
tions of change for all cohorts who travel internation[...]

Regardless of type of international travel, it is cle[...]
travel behavior are due primarily to period effects ([...]
tion of longitudinal and time-lag differences). In [...]
where significant differences were observed, peric[...]
plained the differences. These results are counter to [...]
by Opperman (1995) and You and O'Leary (2000) [...]
ferences between various age groups were cross-sec[...]
ences between younger and older cohorts at one point[...]
With respect to the impact this finding may have on [...]
try, the results suggest that (a) marketers should mo[...]
changes taking place within targeted cohorts, and (b)[...]
should not be based on an assessment of differences [...]
one point in time. Take the example of Baby Boome[...]
begun to monitor aggregate changes within this coh[...]

children, generation to generation" (p. 5). Hence, it is imperative that we account for ethnicity when utilizing forecasting techniques such as cohort analysis (Gobster & Delgado, 1993; Jeong, 1999).

In summary, recognizing that cohorts exhibit distinct patterns of travel behavior is important to the planning and marketing of travel services. However, changes in family structure, introduction of ethnic variations into individuals' perceptions of and involvement in leisure, for example, may also impact travel patterns. Thus, in the future, if marketers want to predict demand for travel services, they should adopt techniques such as Palmore's triad method with various segments of the traveling population (e.g., Asian Americans, Hispanic Americans, extended families, etc.).

REFERENCES

Ambry, M. (1990). How to Age Profitably. *American Demographics*, 12(9): 44.

Archer, B. (1980). Forecasting demand: Quantitative and Intuitive Techniques. *Tourism Management*, 1(March): 5-12.

Archer, B. (1994). Demand Forecasting and Estimation. In J. R. B Ritchie, & C. R. Goeldner (Eds.), *Travel, Tourism and Hospitality Research: A Handbook For Managers and Researchers*, 2nd ed. (pp. 105-114). New York: John Wiley & Sons, Inc.

Baltes, P. B. (1997). On the Incomplete Architecture of Human Ontogeny: Selection, Optimization and Compensation as Foundation of Developmental Theory. *American Psychologist*, 52(4), 366-380.

Barone, M. (2001). *The New Americans: How the Melting Pot Can Work Again*. Washington DC: Regenry Publishing, Inc.

Bonnici, J. L. & Fredenberger, W. B. (1991). Cohort Analysis-A Forecasting Tool. *Journal of Business Forecasting*, 10(3): 9-13.

Crouch, G. (1994). Guidelines for the Study of International Tourism Demand Using Regression Analysis. In B. Ritchie & C. Goeldner (Eds.), *Travel, Tourism and Hospitality Research: A Handbook For Managers* (pp. 583-596). New York: John Wiley & Sons, Inc.

Exter, T. (1986). How to Think About Age. *American Demographics*, 8(9): 50-51.

Foot, D. K. & D. Stoffman. (1997) *Boom, Bust & Echo*. Toronto, Canada: Macfarlane, Walters and Ross, Inc.

Gerber, J., Wolff, J., Klores, W., & Brown, D. (1989). *Life Trends: Your Future For The Next 30 Years*. New York: Avon Books.

Glenn, N. (1977). *Cohort Analysis*. Beverly Hills, CA: Sage.

Gobster, P., & Delgado, A. (1993). Ethnicity and Recreational Use In Chicago's Lincoln Park: In-Park User Survey Findings. In P. Gobster (Ed.), *Managing Urban and High-Use Recreation Settings* (pp. 75-81). General Technical Report NC-163. St. Paul, MN: USDA Forest Service, North Central Experiment Station.

Godbey, G. (1992). *Leisure in America: An Overview.* Manuscript prepared for Takenaka Corporation, Osaka, Japan, April, 1992.

Gunnerson, R. (1986). There's Gold in Seniors. *Target Marketing,* 9: 29 & 21.

Hicks, R. and K. Hicks. (1999). *Boomers, Xers and Other Strangers: Understanding the Generational Differences that Divide Us.* Wheaton, IL: Tyndale House Publishers, Inc.

Jansson, J. (1989). Car Demand Modeling And Forecasting: A New Approach. *Journal of Transport Economics and Policy,* 23(2): 125-140.

Jeong, W. (1999). *Ethnic Variations in Recreational Resource Use: The Case of Asian Immigrants.* Unpublished doctoral dissertation, The Pennsylvania State University, University Park, PA.

Marano, H. (1998). 1999 Outlook On International Tourism. In B. McClure (Ed.), *1999 Outlook for Travel and Tourism* (pp. 252-266). Washington, DC: Travel Industry Association of America.

McPherson, B. D. (1990). *Aging as a Social Process: An Introduction to Individual and Population Aging.* Markham, ONT: Butterworths.

Meredith, G., & Schewe, C. (1994). The Power of Cohorts. *American Demographics,* 16(12): 22-32.

Neumann, W. L. (1997). *Social Research Methods: Qualitative And Quantitative Approaches.* Needham Heights, MA: Allyn & Bacon.

Opperman, M. (1995). Family Life Cycle and Cohort Effects: A Study of Travel Patterns of German Residents. *Journal of Travel & Tourism Marketing,* 4(1): 23-45.

Palmore, E. (1978) When Can Age, Period and Cohort Be Separated? *Social Forces,* 57(1): 282-95.

Pennington-Gray, L. & Kerstetter, D. (2001). Examining Travel Preferences Of Older Canadian Adults Over Time. *Journal of Hospitality and Leisure Marketing,* 8(3/4): 131-146.

Reynolds, F. D. & Rentz, J. O. (1981). Cohort Analysis: An Aid to Strategic Planning. *Journal of Marketing,* 45(summer): 62-70.

Riche, M. (2000). *America's Diversity And Growth: Signposts For The 21st Century.* Washington, DC: Population Reference Bureau.

Riley, M.W., Johnson, M., & Foner, A. (1972). *Aging and Society: A Sociology of Age Stratification.* New York: Russell Sage Foundation.

Ryder, N. (1965). The Cohort as a Concept in the Study of Social Change. *American Sociological Review,* (December): 843-861.

Schaie, W. (1996). Intellectual Development in Aging. In J. Birren and W. Schaie (Eds.), *Handbook of the Psychology of Aging* (pp. 266-286). London: Academic Press Limited.

Simmons Market Research Bureau. (1979-93). *Study of Media and Markets.* New York: Simmons Market Research Bureau.

Singleton, Jr., R., & Straits, B. (1999). *Approaches to Social Research,* 3rd Ed. New York: Oxford University Press.

Smith, S. (1989). *Tourism Analysis: A Handbook.* Essex, England: Longman Scientific & Technical.

Smith, J. W., & Clurman, A. (1997). *Rocking the Ages: The Yankelovich Report on Generational Marketing.* New York: HarperCollins Publishers.

Stoneman, B. (1998). Beyond Rocking The Ages: An Interview with J. Walker Smith. *American Demographics*, (May): 45-49.

Strauss, W., & Howe, N. (1977). *The Fourth Turning: An American Prophecy.* New York: Broadway Books.

Tongren, H. (1988). The Determinant Behavior Characteristics of Older Consumers. *Journal of Consumer Affairs*, 22(1): 136-157.

Travel Industry Association of American (1988). *Discover America 2000: The Implications of America's Changing Demographics and Attitudes on the U.S. Travel Industry.* Washington, D.C.: U.S. Travel Data Center.

Warnick, R. (1993a). *Back To The Future: U.S. Domestic Travel and Generational Trends, 1979 To 1991.* Paper presented at the Resort and Commercial Recreation Association Annual Congress, Mohonk Mountain House, New Paltz, New York, November.

Warnick, R. (1993b). *U.S. Domestic Travel: Back To The Future. The Impacts of An Aging U.S. Population on Domestic Travel Trends.* The Annual Review of Travel (1993 edition) (pp. 75-89). New York: American Express Travel Related Services, Inc.

Weiss, M. (2000). *The Clustered World: How We Live, What We Buy, and What It All Means About Who We Are.* Boston: Little, Brown and Company.

Wolfe, D. (1988). Learning To Speak the Language of The New Senior. *Marketing Communications*, 13(3): 47-52.

World Tourism Organization (1990). *Tourism to the Year 2000: Qualitative Aspects Affecting Global Growth.* Discussion paper, Madrid: World Tourism Organization.

You, X., & O'Leary, J. (2000). Age and Cohort Effects: An Examination of Older Japanese Travelers. *Journal of Travel and Tourism Marketing*, 9(1/2): 21-42.

Young, C., & Smith, R. (1979). Aggregated and Disaggregated Outdoor Recreation Participation Models. *Leisure Sciences*, 2: 143-154.

Index

SPECIAL 25%-OFF DISCOUNT!

Order a copy of this book with this form or online at
http://www.haworthpress.com/store/product.asp?sku=4875
Use Sale Code BOF25 in the online bookshop to receive 25% off!

Tourism Forecasting and Marketing

____ in softbound at $18.71 (regularly $24.95) (ISBN: 0-7890-2087-4)
____ in hardbound at $37.46 (regularly $49.95) (ISBN: 0-7890-2086-6)

COST OF BOOKS _____

Outside USA/ Canada/
Mexico: Add 20% _____

POSTAGE & HANDLING _____
(US: $4.00 for first book & $1.50
for each additional book)
Outside US: $5.00 for first book
& $2.00 for each additional book)

SUBTOTAL _____

in Canada: add 7% GST _____

STATE TAX _____
(NY, OH, & MIN residents please
add appropriate local sales tax)

FINAL TOTAL _____
(if paying in Canadian funds, convert
using the current exchange rate,
UNESCO coupons welcome)

☐ BILL ME LATER: ($5 service charge will be added)
(Bill-me option is good on US/Canada/
Mexico orders only; not good to jobbers,
wholesalers, or subscription agencies.)

☐ Signature _____

☐ Payment Enclosed: $ _____

☐ PLEASE CHARGE TO MY CREDIT CARD:

☐ Visa ☐ MasterCard ☐ AmEx ☐ Discover
☐ Diner's Club ☐ Eurocard ☐ JCB

Account #_____

Exp Date _____

Signature_____
(Prices in US dollars and subject to
change without notice.)

PLEASE PRINT ALL INFORMATION OR ATTACH YOUR BUSINESS CARD

Name		
Address		
City	State/Province	Zip/Postal Code
Country		
Tel	Fax	
E-Mail		

May we use your e-mail address for confirmations and other types of information? ☐Yes ☐No
We appreciate receiving your e-mail address and fax number. Haworth would like to e-mail or
fax special discount offers to you, as a preferred customer. **We will never share, rent, or
exchange your e-mail address or fax number.** We regard such actions as an invasion of
your privacy.

Order From Your Local Bookstore or Directly From
The Haworth Press, Inc.
10 Alice Street, Binghamton, New York 13904-1580 • USA
Call Our toll-free number (1-800-429-6784) / Outside US/Canada: (607) 722-5857
Fax: 1-800-895-0582 / Outside US/Canada: (607) 771-0012
E-Mail your order to us: Orders@haworthpress.com

Please Photocopy this form for your personal use.
www.HaworthPress.com

BOF03